Barb

merry Christmas 20
to my dear friend

xoxoxo
Silver

THE
SOUTHERN
BAKER

THE
SOUTHERN
BAKER

Sweet and Savory Treats to Share with Friends and Family

By the Editors of Southern Living

OXMOOR
HOUSE®

CONTENTS

THE RECIPES WE CHERISH

Every Southern baker I have ever met has at least one precious recipe, handed down to him or her from generations before. Made over and over again, year after year, often completely from memory, the recipe is refined and the hands are trained to create this sweet offering ever so perfectly. With a knowing grin, the baker presents it at gatherings and holidays, waiting for the first bite to overwhelm each guest, bringing that unmistakable look of happiness.

Whether a humble treat made on a busy weeknight or a heart-stopping, gorgeous masterpiece, each recipe carries with it a piece of our history along with a generous helping of pure love. While there are endless recipes available, some stand the test of time in our minds and in our hearts. This book is brimming with the recipes that every Southern baker should know. Tested again and again, these are the stars, the desserts worth celebrating, the treats you can't forget.

Some bakers keep their prized recipes closely guarded—maybe even treasured as a family secret—but here at *Southern Living* we want to share every last bit of advice, each and every baking secret, and all our beloved recipes with you, so that they may soon become your family's cherished heirlooms.

Happy Baking!

Allison Cox Vasquez

Allison Cox Vasquez
Editor

EQUIPMENT & TOOLS

*Baking up gorgeous treats is easy as pie if you
have all the right equipment and tools at the ready.*

small appliances

A **heavy-duty electric stand mixer** comes with attachments: a paddle, a dough hook, and a whisk-like wire beater. A **handheld electric mixer** is perfect for mixing lighter batters or using with a double boiler on the cooktop. A large **food processor** makes easy work of chopping nuts and chocolate, as well as mixing up homemade piecrusts.

equipment

Mixing bowls are essential in any kitchen and come in a range of sizes, including small prep bowls. Use glass bowls for microwaving. **Baking sheets** are a necessity. A jelly-roll pan has shallow sides for making sponge cakes. A cookie sheet does not have raised sides. **Muffin and loaf pans** are available in nonstick, steel, or aluminum and come with 6 or 12 cups, varying from miniature to jumbo sizes. It's a great idea to have a variety of sizes of loaf pans from 5 x 3 inches to 9 x 5 inches. **Pie plates** come in glass, ceramic, or metal and are available in 9-inch, 10-inch, and deep-dish sizes. **Tart pans** are shallow with fluted sides and can be round, square, or rectangular; common sizes are 10 inches and 11 inches. **Cake pans** are helpful to have in sets of three in at least two sizes, 8 inches and 9 inches. Other useful specialty cake pans are a **Bundt pan**, a **tube pan, 13- x 9-inch pan**, and a **springform pan**. A **wire cooling rack** allows air to circulate evenly on all sides of freshly baked cakes, pies, or cookies.

helpful tools

Dry measuring cups come as a set of graduated cups ranging from ¼ cup to 1 cup; they're usually made from plastic or metal. **Liquid measuring cups** are generally made from glass and have a pouring spout. **Nested measuring spoons** come in a set of graduated sizes that range from ⅛ tsp. to 1 Tbsp. **Rubber spatulas** in small, medium, and large are helpful to scrape batters from bowls into baking pans or to spread fillings. **Wooden spoons** are perfect for stirring heavy or dense mixtures. **Wire whisks** come in varying sizes and shapes that are great for custards or creams. A **rolling pin** is a must-have, whether a traditional one with 2 handles or a French tapered one. **Cookie scoops**, available in a variety of sizes, are perfect for scooping muffin batter into pans or cookie dough onto baking sheets. A **piecrust shield** is placed over a pie while baking to prevent over-browning. A **pastry brush** is great for brushing crumbs from a cake or coating dough with egg wash or melted butter. A **candy thermometer** allows you to cook mixtures to precise temperatures. **Ceramic pie weights** prevent a prebaked piecrust from forming large air bubbles. A **box grater** and **Microplane grater** make easy work of shredding cheeses and frozen butter or zesting citrus fruits and finely grating chocolate. A **wire sifter** removes lumps from flour or powdered sugar.

INGREDIENTS

Get ready to bake up a storm with a pantry stocked full of the ingredients you should always have on hand.

flours

All-purpose flour is great for most baked goods such as cookies, piecrusts, quick breads, and some cakes. **Cake flour** has less protein (gluten) than all-purpose flour and creates a very tender crumb in biscuits or light cakes. **Bread flour** has the most protein (gluten) of widely available flours, and as its name suggests, it's perfect for breads and also pizza doughs. **Whole wheat flour** is nice to substitute for some of the all-purpose flour in a recipe. It gives a nutty, wholesome flavor, without making treats too dense.

sweeteners

Granulated sugar or white sugar is the most common sugar in the U.S. and is made from sugar cane or sugar beets. **Brown sugar** is made by adding a little bit of molasses to white granulated sugar, which gives it more flavor. Depending on the amount of molasses added, dark or light brown sugar is created. **Molasses** is a dark, sweet syrup with intense flavor made from sugar cane. Its dark richness and acidity give baked goods a deep, truly Southern flavor. **Cane syrup** is lighter syrup made from sugar cane that has a clean, honey-like flavor. **Light corn syrup** has the least flavor but highest sweetening ability of syrups. **Dark corn syrup** is brown in color and has a caramel-like flavor. **Honey** and **maple syrup** are both syrups made in nature, and each has a distinct but light flavor, depending on the grade and variety purchased.

fats

Butter is made from extracting all the flavorful fat from heavy cream and a bit of salt too. It adds richness and tenderness to baked goods but has a lower melting point and burning point than other fats. **Shortening** is a solid fat made from vegetable oil. It is the most stable of fats but imparts little flavor to baked goods. It's perfect for greasing pans and making flaky doughs. **Vegetable oil** has a mild flavor, making it great for frying or as an ingredient in dense cakes or brownies.

dairy

Heavy cream is a favorite among bakers because it can be whipped up into a cloud or stirred in to add velvety richness. Look for the highest fat cream for added stability and flavor. **Buttermilk** is a cultured cow's milk that adds a little acidity to baked goods and fillings. Its distinct flavor and versatility make it a staple in Southern kitchens. **Whole eggs** give baked goods stability, lift, and flavor, thanks to their unique combination of protein and fat. We tested with large eggs in all our recipes.

risen breads
& rolls

RISEN BREADS

Follow these basic steps and your bread will rise to the occasion.

Don't be intimidated by yeast; embrace it. A friendly fungus, yeast is the microscopic magic that leavens bread and gives it its unique texture and flavor. At the grocery store, you'll see instant (or "rapid-rise") and active dry yeast. We recommend active dry—the activation (Step 2, below) means the yeast is alive and ready to go to work. Then be sure to knead dough and allow to fully rise, according to your recipe. For loaves, this simple shaping technique ensures the perfect texture that's optimal for slicing baked bread.

·······*activating & mixing*·······

Step 1: Use yeast packets before the expiration date. To store yeast after it has been opened, refrigerate the granules in an airtight container.

Step 2: Stir active dry yeast into warm water (100° to 110°). Too cold and the granules will remain dormant; too hot and the yeast will die.

Step 3: Yeast loves sugar, so add a pinch to speed up activation. If bubbles appear after 5 minutes, you're golden. That's the gas that makes bread rise.

Step 4: Combine yeast mixture with other dough ingredients, generally flour, oil, salt, and often eggs, sugar, and milk, depending on the recipe.

·······*kneading & rising*·······

Step 5: Add all but a cup of remaining flour, mixing until completely incorporated.

Step 6: Gradually add remaining flour until a soft dough forms.

Step 7: Continue mixing until dough is smooth and all the flour is incorporated.

Step 8: Turn out dough onto a floured surface.

Step 9: Sprinkle surface of dough with flour as needed to work.

Step 10: Knead dough until smooth and elastic, about 8 to 10 minutes.

Step 11: Cover and let rise in a warm place (80° to 85°), free from drafts, about 1 hour or until doubled in bulk.

Step 12: Punch dough down to release trapped air; turn out onto a lightly floured surface.

.... *shaping & baking* ....

Step 13: For recipes that make 2 loaves, divide dough in half evenly using a bench knife or pastry scraper.

Step 14: Roll each dough half evenly into an 18- x 9-inch rectangle.

Step 15: Starting at 1 of the short ends, tightly roll each rectangle, jelly-roll fashion. Pinch ends of dough to seal, and tuck ends under dough.

Step 16: Place each dough roll, seam side down, in a lightly greased loaf pan.

Step 17: Brush tops of loaves with oil, butter, or an egg wash to achieve a golden brown crust.

Step 18: Cover and let rise in a warm place (80° to 85°), free from drafts, 1 hour or until doubled in bulk.

Step 19: Bake loaves according to recipe directions, until golden brown and have a hollow sound when tapped.

Step 20: Transfer loaves to a wire rack, and brush with melted butter. Let cool completely before slicing.

NEW ORLEANS CALAS

The Calas Women, as they were called, peddled these hot breakfast fritters—whose name comes from the African word kárá— each morning in the French Quarter. Long departed, we honor them here with a classic rice-dough recipe too delicious to ever disappear.

makes about 2½ dozen calas   hands-on 45 min.   total 10 hours, 10 min.

½   cup uncooked medium-grain rice
¾   tsp. table salt, divided
½   cup warm water (100° to 110°)
1¼ tsp. active dry yeast
1   tsp. granulated sugar
3   large eggs, lightly beaten

1¼ cups all-purpose flour
¼   cup granulated sugar
¼   tsp. ground nutmeg
    Vegetable oil
    Powdered sugar

1. Bring 6 cups water to a boil in a saucepan over medium-high heat. Stir in rice and ¼ tsp. salt. Reduce heat to medium, and cook, stirring often, 25 to 30 minutes. (Rice will be very soft and thick.) Remove from heat, and drain. Place 1½ cups cooked rice in a bowl, discarding remaining rice. Mash rice with a potato masher 30 seconds. Cool 20 minutes or until lukewarm.

2. Stir together warm water, yeast, and 1 tsp. granulated sugar in a 1-cup glass measuring cup; let stand 5 minutes. Stir yeast mixture into rice. Cover with plastic wrap, and let stand in a warm place (80° to 85°), free from drafts, 8 to 12 hours.

3. Stir eggs into rice mixture. Combine flour, next 2 ingredients, and remaining ½ tsp. salt. Stir flour mixture into rice mixture. Cover with plastic wrap, and let stand in a warm place (80° to 85°), free from drafts, 30 minutes.

4. Meanwhile, pour oil to depth of 3 inches into a deep cast-iron skillet or large Dutch oven; heat to 350°. Drop dough by rounded tablespoonfuls into hot oil, and fry, in batches, 3 minutes or until golden brown. Drain on paper towels. Sprinkle with powdered sugar, and serve immediately.

Note: We tested with Water Maid Medium-Grain Enriched Rice.

⁓⁂⁂ BAKING SECRETS ⁂⁂⁓
from the Southern Living Test Kitchen

The best place to let the rice mixture rise free of drafts is inside your oven. Be sure it's cooled down if you were baking in it recently, and certainly don't turn on your oven while the mixture is inside!

oranges

How do you tell the difference between a Florida orange
and a California orange? California oranges tend to have
a golden orange-yellow color and a thick, even skin.
Florida oranges range in color from orange to orange-yellow
to greenish-yellow and tend to have a thinner skin.

ORANGE ROLLS

The rolls need rising time, so plan this recipe for a weekend or day off.

makes 24 servings   hands-on 30 min.   total 3 hours, 30 min., including topping and glaze

1	(¼-oz.) envelope active dry yeast	4½	cups bread flour
½	cup plus 1 tsp. granulated sugar, divided	¼	tsp. ground nutmeg
¼	cup warm water (100° to 110°)	¼	to ½ cup bread flour
1	cup butter, softened and divided	1⅓	cups powdered sugar
1	tsp. table salt	¼	cup honey
2	large eggs, lightly beaten	2	large egg whites
1	cup milk	1	cup coarsely chopped pecans (optional)
1	Tbsp. fresh lemon juice		Fresh Orange Glaze

1. Combine yeast, 1 tsp. granulated sugar, and warm water in a small bowl; let stand 5 minutes.

2. Beat ½ cup butter at medium speed with a heavy-duty electric stand mixer, using paddle attachment, until creamy. Gradually add remaining ½ cup granulated sugar and salt, beating until light and fluffy. Add eggs, milk, and lemon juice, beating until blended. Stir in yeast mixture.

3. Combine 4½ cups bread flour and nutmeg. Gradually add to butter mixture, beating at low speed 2 minutes or until well blended.

4. Turn dough out onto a surface floured with about ¼ cup bread flour; knead for 5 minutes, adding additional bread flour as needed. Place dough in a lightly greased large bowl, turning to grease top of dough. Cover and let rise in a warm place (80° to 85°), free from drafts, 1½ to 2 hours or until doubled in bulk.

5. Punch dough down; turn out onto a lightly floured surface. Divide dough in half. Divide one dough half into 12 equal pieces; shape each piece, rolling between hands, into a 7- to 8-inch-long rope. Wrap each rope into a coil, firmly pinching end to seal. Place rolls in a lightly greased 10-inch round cake pan. Repeat procedure with remaining dough half. Melt remaining ½ cup butter in a medium bowl. Stir in powdered sugar, honey, and egg whites until smooth; drizzle half of topping evenly over each pan of rolls.

6. Let rise, uncovered, in a warm place (80° to 85°), free from drafts, 1 hour or until doubled in bulk. Top evenly with pecans, if desired.

7. Preheat oven to 350°. Bake at 350° for 20 to 22 minutes or until rolls are lightly browned. Cool rolls 2 minutes in pans. Spoon half of Fresh Orange Glaze evenly over each pan of warm rolls, and serve immediately.

FRESH ORANGE GLAZE

2	cups powdered sugar	3	Tbsp. fresh orange juice
2	Tbsp. butter, softened	1	Tbsp. fresh lemon juice
2	tsp. orange zest		

Beat powdered sugar and butter at medium speed with an electric mixer until blended. Add remaining ingredients, and beat until smooth. **Makes ¾ cup.**

CARAMEL APPLE FANTANS

At the turn of the 20th century, the South was the apple capital of the world.
This recipe celebrates the autumn fruit. Use any firm cooking apple, such as 'Jonagold'
or 'Honeycrisp,' or seek out Southern heirlooms, like 'Terry Winter' or 'Yellow June.'

makes 1 dozen fantans   hands-on 50 min.   total 2 hours, 45 min.

Dough:
1	(¼-oz.) envelope active dry yeast
1	cup warm water (100° to 110°)
1	tsp. granulated sugar
1	large egg
¼	cup granulated sugar
¼	cup butter, melted
1	tsp. table salt
1½ to 2	cups bread flour
1½	cups whole wheat flour

Filling:
9	Tbsp. butter, softened and divided
3	cups peeled and diced Braeburn apples (about 3 large)
½	cup golden raisins
¼	cup firmly packed light brown sugar
¾	cup granulated sugar
1	Tbsp. ground cinnamon
¾	cup toasted chopped pecans

Glaze:
⅓	cup butter
⅓	cup firmly packed light brown sugar

1. Prepare Dough: Combine first 3 ingredients in bowl of a heavy-duty electric stand mixer; let stand 5 minutes. Stir in egg, next 3 ingredients, and 1½ cups bread flour. Beat at medium speed, using paddle attachment, 1 minute or until smooth. Gradually beat in whole wheat flour and enough remaining bread flour to make a soft dough. Turn dough out onto a well-floured surface, and knead until smooth and elastic (6 to 8 minutes), sprinkling surface with bread flour as needed. Place dough in a lightly greased large bowl, turning to grease top. Cover with plastic wrap, and let rise in a warm place (80° to 85°), free from drafts, 45 to 55 minutes or until doubled in bulk.

2. Meanwhile, prepare Filling: Melt 1 Tbsp. butter in a large skillet over medium-high heat. Add apples and next 2 ingredients, and sauté 4 to 5 minutes or until apples are crisp-tender. Cool completely (about 30 minutes).

3. Punch dough down; turn out onto a lightly floured surface. Roll into a 20- x 12-inch rectangle. Spread remaining 8 Tbsp. softened butter over dough. Stir together ¾ cup granulated sugar and cinnamon; sprinkle over butter, and top with pecans and apple mixture.

4. Cut dough into 5 (12- x 4-inch) strips; stack dough strips. Replace any apples and pecans that fall out. Cut stack into 6 (4- x 2-inch) rectangles; cut each rectangle in half crosswise to form 12 (2-inch) squares. Place stacked squares, cut sides up, into cups of a lightly greased 12-cup muffin pan. Cover loosely with plastic wrap; let rise in a warm place (80° to 85°), free from drafts, 45 minutes to 1 hour or until rolls rise about ¾ inch above rim of pan.

5. Preheat oven to 375°. Bake at 375° for 18 to 20 minutes or until deep golden brown. Cool in pan on a wire rack 5 minutes. Remove from pan to wire rack.

6. Prepare Glaze: Bring ⅓ cup butter and ⅓ cup brown sugar to a boil in a 1-qt. heavy saucepan over medium heat, stirring constantly; boil 1 minute, stirring constantly. Remove from heat; drizzle over top of warm rolls.

ICED CINNAMON ROLLS

Cream cheese adds richness and body to the icing
spread on these warm breakfast favorites.

makes 16 rolls   hands-on 30 min.   total 3 hours, 40 min.

1	(¼-oz.) envelope active dry yeast	1	Tbsp. fresh lemon juice
¼	cup warm water (100° to 110°)	¼	tsp. ground nutmeg
1	tsp. granulated sugar	4½	cups bread flour
1	cup butter, softened, divided	¼	to ½ cup bread flour
1	cup granulated sugar, divided	½	cup firmly packed light brown sugar
1	tsp. table salt	1	Tbsp. ground cinnamon
2	large eggs, lightly beaten	1	cup toasted chopped pecans
1	cup milk		Cream Cheese Icing

1. Combine first 3 ingredients in a 1-cup glass measuring cup; let stand 5 minutes.

2. Beat ½ cup butter at medium speed with a heavy-duty electric stand mixer until creamy. Gradually add ½ cup granulated sugar and table salt, beating at medium speed until light and fluffy. Add eggs and next 3 ingredients, beating until blended. Stir in yeast mixture.

3. Gradually add 4½ cups flour to butter mixture, beating at low speed 1 to 2 minutes or until well blended.

4. Sprinkle about ¼ cup bread flour onto a flat surface; turn dough out, and knead until smooth and elastic (about 5 minutes), adding up to ¼ cup bread flour as needed to prevent dough from sticking to hands and surface. Place dough in a lightly greased large bowl, turning to grease top. Cover and let rise in a warm place (80° to 85°), free from drafts, 1½ to 2 hours or until doubled in bulk.

5. Punch dough down; turn out onto a lightly floured surface. Roll into a 16- x 12-inch rectangle. Spread with remaining ½ cup butter, leaving a 1-inch border around edges. Stir together brown sugar, cinnamon, and remaining ½ cup granulated sugar, and sprinkle sugar mixture over butter. Top with pecans. Roll up dough, jelly-roll fashion, starting at 1 long side; cut into 16 slices.

6. Place rolls, cut sides down, in 2 lightly greased 10-inch round pans. Cover and let rise in a warm place (80° to 85°), free from drafts, 1 hour or until doubled in bulk.

7. Preheat oven to 350°. Bake at 350° for 20 to 22 minutes or until rolls are golden brown. Cool in pans 5 minutes. Brush rolls with Cream Cheese Icing. Serve immediately.

CREAM CHEESE ICING

1	(3-oz.) package cream cheese, softened	1	tsp. vanilla extract
2	Tbsp. butter, softened	2	Tbsp. milk
2¼	cups powdered sugar		

Beat first 2 ingredients at medium speed with an electric mixer until creamy. Gradually add powdered sugar, beating at low speed until blended. Stir in vanilla and 1 Tbsp. milk. Add remaining 1 Tbsp. milk, 1 tsp. at a time, stirring until icing is smooth and creamy. **Makes 1½ cups.**

CHOCOLATE BREAKFAST WREATH

From Virginia to Atlanta, artisanal chocolate makers are popping up all over the South. Look to their products to infuse this holiday wreath with authentic regional flavor. Be sure to soften the butter until it's spreadable. The silky dough is a dream to work with, so even beginning bakers can make this beautiful wreath.

makes 10 to 12 servings   hands-on 25 min.   total 3 hours, 40 min., including glaze

½ cup warm milk (100° to 110°)
2 (¼-oz.) envelopes active dry yeast
⅓ cup plus ½ cup sugar, divided
4½ cups all-purpose flour, divided
2 tsp. kosher salt
1½ cups soft butter, divided

3 large eggs, at room temperature
Parchment paper
1 (4-oz.) bittersweet chocolate baking bar, finely chopped
Easy Vanilla Glaze

1. Combine milk, yeast, and ⅓ cup sugar in bowl of a heavy-duty electric stand mixer; let stand 5 minutes or until foamy. Gradually add 1 cup flour, beating at low speed until blended; scrape down sides. Add salt and 1 cup butter; beat at low speed until smooth. Add eggs, 1 at a time, beating until blended after each addition and scraping sides of bowl as needed. Gradually add remaining 3½ cups flour, beating until blended. Increase speed to medium, and beat until dough forms a ball and begins to pull away from sides. Beat dough 2 more minutes or until smooth and elastic. Turn dough out onto a lightly floured surface, and knead 3 minutes.

2. Place dough in a greased large bowl, turning to grease top. Cover with plastic wrap, and let rise in a warm place (80° to 85°), free from drafts, 1 hour or until doubled in bulk. Punch dough down, and turn out onto lightly floured parchment paper. Roll dough into an 18- x 12-inch rectangle.

3. Brush 6 Tbsp. soft butter over dough; sprinkle with chocolate and ½ cup sugar. Roll up dough, jelly-roll fashion, starting at 1 long side. Press edge to seal, and place dough, seam side down, on parchment paper.

4. Transfer parchment paper with dough onto a baking sheet. Shape rolled dough into a ring, pressing ends together to seal. Cut ring at 2-inch intervals, from outer edge up to (but not through) inside edge. Gently pull and twist cut pieces to show filling. Cover dough.

5. Let rise in a warm place (80° to 85°), free from drafts, 1 hour or until doubled in bulk. Preheat oven to 350°. Uncover dough. Melt remaining 2 Tbsp. butter; brush over dough. Bake at 350° for 30 to 40 minutes or until golden. Cool on pan 10 minutes. Drizzle Easy Vanilla Glaze over warm bread.

EASY VANILLA GLAZE

2 cups powdered sugar
3 to 4 Tbsp. milk

½ tsp. vanilla extract
Dash of table salt

Whisk together powdered sugar, 3 Tbsp. milk, vanilla, and salt. Whisk in up to 1 Tbsp. milk, 1 tsp. at a time, to reach desired consistency. **Makes 1½ cups.**

26

HAM-AND-SWISS STICKY BUNS

Stuff the dough deep into the muffin tin so that the tops rise into a cheesy dome while baking.

makes 16 rolls   hands-on 20 min.   total 1 hour, 10 min.

9   oz. deli ham, finely chopped
2   cups (8 oz.) shredded Swiss cheese
2   Tbsp. spicy brown mustard
½   cup firmly packed light brown sugar

2   (16.3-oz.) cans refrigerated
    jumbo biscuits
Maple syrup

1. Preheat oven to 325°. Stir together first 3 ingredients.

2. Sprinkle brown sugar into a 12-inch square on a clean surface. Arrange biscuits in 4 rows on sugar, covering sugar completely. Pinch biscuits together to form a square. Roll dough into a 16- x 12-inch rectangle (about ¼ inch thick), pinching dough together as needed. Spread ham-and-cheese mixture over dough. Roll up tightly, starting at 1 long side, pressing brown sugar into dough as you roll. Pinch ends to seal. Cut into 16 slices using a serrated knife. Fit each slice into cups of a lightly greased 24-cup muffin pan. (Dough will extend over tops of cups.)

3. Bake at 325° for 40 minutes or until golden and centers are completely cooked. Cool on a wire rack 10 minutes. Drizzle with syrup.

Note: We tested with Pillsbury Grands! Flaky Layers Original refrigerated biscuits.

xxxxxxxxxxxxxxxxxxxxxxxxxxxxxxxxxxxx

time-saving tip

To make ahead, prepare recipe through Step 2, and chill
8 hours. Let stand 10 minutes. Proceed as directed in Step 3.

xxxxxxxxxxxxxxxxxxxxxxxxxxxxxxxxxxxx

CARAMEL-GLAZED MONKEY BREAD

We'd wager our presents under the tree that this is the best pull-apart bread on Earth. The dough is soft and cakey, and the loaf dons a scrumptious sugary crust.

makes 10 to 12 servings   hands-on 30 min.   total 5 hours, 5 min.

Wax paper

Dough:
- ½   cup warm water (100° to 110°)
- 1   (¼-oz.) envelope active dry yeast
- 1   tsp. sugar
- 5   cups all-purpose flour
- 3   Tbsp. sugar
- 5   tsp. baking powder
- 1½   tsp. table salt
- 1   tsp. baking soda
- ½   cup cold butter, cubed
- ½   cup shortening, cubed
- 2   cups buttermilk, at room temperature

Coating:
- ¾   cup granulated sugar
- ¾   cup firmly packed light brown sugar
- 1   Tbsp. ground cinnamon
- ¾   cup butter, melted
- 1   cup toasted chopped pecans

Glaze:
- ¾   cup firmly packed light brown sugar
- 6   Tbsp. butter
- 3   Tbsp. milk
- 1   tsp. vanilla extract

1. Generously grease a 10-inch (12-cup) tube pan; line bottom with wax paper, and lightly grease wax paper.

2. Prepare Dough: Stir together first 3 ingredients in a 1-cup glass measuring cup; let stand 5 minutes.

3. Stir together flour and next 4 ingredients in a large bowl; cut butter and shortening into flour mixture with a pastry blender or 2 forks until crumbly. Add yeast mixture and buttermilk, stirring just until dry ingredients are moistened. Cover with plastic wrap, and chill 2 to 72 hours.

4. Prepare Coating: Stir together granulated sugar and next 2 ingredients in a small bowl. Turn dough out onto a lightly floured surface, and knead 3 or 4 times. Shape dough into about 60 (1½-inch) balls. Dip each in melted butter; roll in sugar mixture.

5. Place a single layer of coated balls in prepared pan, covering bottom completely. Sprinkle with ⅓ cup pecans. Repeat layers twice. Top with any remaining sugar mixture; drizzle with any remaining melted butter.

6. Cover dough; let stand 1 hour.

7. Preheat oven to 350°. Uncover and bake at 350° for 40 to 45 minutes or until a wooden pick inserted in center comes out clean. Transfer to a wire rack, and cool 20 minutes. Remove from pan to wire rack, discarding wax paper. Invert onto a serving platter.

8. Meanwhile, prepare Glaze: Bring first 3 ingredients to a boil in a small saucepan over medium heat, stirring constantly; boil, stirring constantly, 1 minute. Remove from heat, and stir in vanilla. Stir constantly 2 minutes. Drizzle bread with glaze. Serve warm.

Spoon Rolls

Refrigerator
Yeast Rolls

Potato-Caramelized
Onion Buns

Two-Seed
Bread Knots

SPOON ROLLS

(pictured on page 30)

These can be baked in any well-greased muffin pan, but as with cornbread, the cast iron creates a wonderfully crisp crust. If you're a fan of muffin tops, try baking these rolls in a drop biscuit pan.

makes 14 rolls   hands-on 15 min.   total 40 min.

1   (¼-oz.) envelope active dry yeast
2   cups warm water (100° to 110°)
4   cups self-rising flour

¼   cup sugar
¾   cup butter, melted
1   large egg, lightly beaten

1. Preheat oven to 400°. Combine yeast and 2 cups warm water in a large bowl; let mixture stand 5 minutes.

2. Stir in flour and remaining ingredients until blended. Spoon into well-greased cast-iron muffin pans, filling two-thirds full, or into well-greased cast-iron drop biscuit pans, filling half full.

3. Bake at 400° for 20 minutes or until rolls are golden brown.

×××××××××××××××××××××××××××××××××××××

time-saving tip

Unused batter may be stored in an airtight container in the refrigerator for up to 1 week. Bake up the exact amount of rolls you need, and save the rest of the batter for later.

×××××××××××××××××××××××××××××××××××××

REFRIGERATOR YEAST ROLLS

(pictured on page 30)

Some bread recipes require a serious time commitment. These rolls, however, are designed to save you time by letting the dough rise in the refrigerator overnight. Then all you have to do is shape the rolls, give them a quick rise, and bake.

makes about 7 dozen rolls   hands-on 45 min.   total 9 hours, 45 min.

1 (¼-oz.) envelope active dry yeast	½ tsp. table salt
2 cups warm water (100° to 110°)	½ cup shortening
6 cups bread flour	2 large eggs
½ cup sugar	½ cup butter, melted

1. Stir together yeast and warm water in a medium bowl; let mixture stand 5 minutes.

2. Stir together flour, sugar, and salt in a large bowl. Cut shortening into flour mixture with a pastry blender until crumbly; stir in yeast mixture and eggs just until blended. (Do not overmix.) Cover and chill 8 hours.

3. Roll dough to ¼-inch thickness on a well-floured surface (dough will be soft); cut with a 1½-inch round cutter, rerolling dough scraps as needed.

4. Brush rounds with melted butter. Make a crease across each round with a knife, and fold rounds in half, gently pressing edges together to seal. Place in a 15- x 10-inch jelly-roll pan and a 9-inch round cake pan. (Edges of dough should touch.) Cover and let rise in a warm place (80° to 85°), free from drafts, 45 minutes or until doubled in bulk.

5. Preheat oven to 400°. Bake rolls at 400° for 8 to 10 minutes or until golden.

BAKING SECRETS
from the Southern Living Test Kitchen

Not all yeasts work the same way. This recipe calls for active dry yeast, the kind that should be dissolved and activated in warm water before mixing into the other ingredients. On the other hand, rapid-rise yeast can be mixed directly into dry ingredients and then combined with the warmed liquids.

POTATO~CARAMELIZED ONION BUNS

(pictured on page 31)

We added caramelized onions to this wonderful potato bread recipe.
Serve meaty cheeseburgers or grilled fish inside these delicious buns.

makes about 2 dozen   hands-on 45 min.   total 2 hours, 50 min.

2   cups warm water (100° to 110°)

3   (¼-oz.) envelopes active dry yeast

1   cup refrigerated or frozen mashed
    potatoes, thawed and warmed

2   Tbsp. sugar

2   Tbsp. butter, melted

7   cups plus 1 Tbsp. all-purpose flour

1   Tbsp. table salt

Caramelized Onions

Parchment paper

1   large egg, lightly beaten

1½ tsp. poppy seeds (optional)

1. Preheat oven to 200°. Stir together 2 cups warm water and yeast in bowl of a heavy-duty electric stand mixer until dissolved. Let stand 5 minutes.

2. Add potatoes, sugar, and butter to yeast mixture; beat at medium speed, using dough hook attachment, until blended. Add 7 cups flour and salt; beat at low speed 2 minutes. Add Caramelized Onions, and beat at medium speed 5 minutes. (Dough will be very sticky.) Sprinkle dough with remaining 1 Tbsp. flour, and remove from bowl.

3. Shape into a ball, and place in a lightly greased bowl, turning to grease top. Turn off oven. Cover bowl with plastic wrap, and let rise in oven 30 minutes or until doubled in bulk.

4. Remove from oven. Remove and discard plastic wrap. Punch dough down, and turn out onto a lightly floured surface. Divide into 24 portions.

5. Preheat oven to 350°. Shape each portion into a ball, using floured hands. Place no more than 8 balls on each parchment paper-lined baking sheet. Cover with plastic wrap, and let rise again in a warm place (80° to 85°), free from drafts, for 15 to 20 minutes or until doubled in bulk. Brush with egg, and sprinkle with poppy seeds, if desired.

6. Bake buns at 350° for 15 to 18 minutes or until golden brown. Remove from pans, and cool on wire racks.

CARAMELIZED ONIONS

¼   cup butter

2   large sweet onions, chopped

½   tsp. table salt

Melt butter in a large skillet over medium heat; add onions and salt, and sauté 20 minutes or until caramel colored. Cool. **Makes 2 cups.**

TWO~SEED BREAD KNOTS

(pictured on page 31)

These seeded rolls get their deep golden brown color thanks to the egg yolk that's brushed over them before baking; it does double duty by serving as the adhesive for the sesame and poppy seeds adorning the tops.

makes 20 rolls   hands-on 30 min.   total 1 hour, 5 min.

1 (¼-oz.) envelope active dry yeast	3 Tbsp. olive oil
1 cup warm water (100° to 110°)	1 large egg yolk
3½ cups bread flour	1 Tbsp. sesame seeds
2 Tbsp. sugar	1 tsp. poppy seeds
1½ tsp. table salt	Parchment paper

1. Preheat oven to 200°. Combine yeast and 1 cup warm water in a 2-cup liquid measuring cup; let mixture stand 5 minutes.

2. Combine flour, sugar, and salt in bowl of a heavy-duty electric stand mixer. Add yeast mixture and oil. Beat at low speed 1 minute; beat at medium speed 5 minutes.

3. Divide dough into 20 equal portions. Shape each portion into a 7-inch rope, and shape into a knot. Combine egg yolk and 1 Tbsp. water; brush over rolls. Sprinkle with seeds; place on parchment paper-lined baking sheets. Turn oven off, cover rolls loosely with plastic wrap; place in oven, and let rise 15 to 20 minutes or until doubled in bulk. Remove from oven, and preheat oven to 400°. Discard plastic wrap.

4. Bake at 400° for 15 to 17 minutes or until golden.

xxxxxxxxxxxxxxxxxxxxxxxxxxxxxxxxxxxx

sweet idea

Serve these beautiful rolls for dinner in a basket covered
with a towel to keep them warm, and whip up some
garlic-herb butter to serve alongside. Just stir together ½ cup
softened butter, 2 minced garlic cloves, ¼ tsp. freshly ground
black pepper, ¼ tsp. sea salt, and 1 Tbsp. chopped fresh parsley.

xxxxxxxxxxxxxxxxxxxxxxxxxxxxxxxxxxxx

BLUEBERRY KOLACHES

Originating from central Europe, these rolls were brought to the Hill Country of Texas by immigrants. Considered the unofficial "breakfast pastry of Texas," these are stuffed with fresh blueberries or mango and topped with a sweet crumble.

makes about 3 dozen kolaches   hands-on 40 min.   total 10 hours, 5 min.

1 (¼-oz.) envelope active dry yeast
½ cup warm water (100° to 110°)
½ cup butter, softened
1⅓ cups sugar
2½ tsp. table salt
2 large eggs
8½ cups all-purpose flour

2 cups milk
3 (6-oz.) containers fresh blueberries (about 3 cups)
⅓ cup blueberry preserves
⅓ cup all-purpose flour
⅓ cup sugar
3 Tbsp. cold butter, cut up

1. Combine yeast and warm water in a bowl; let stand 5 minutes.

2. Beat butter at medium speed with an electric mixer until creamy; gradually add 1⅓ cups sugar and 2½ tsp. salt. Add eggs, 1 at a time, beating just until blended after each addition. Stir in yeast mixture.

3. Add 8½ cups flour to butter mixture alternately with milk, beginning and ending with flour mixture. Beat at low speed just until blended, stopping to scrape bowl as needed. Place dough in a well-greased bowl, turning to grease top. Cover with plastic wrap, and chill 8 to 24 hours.

4. Shape dough into 35 (2-inch) balls (about ¼ cup per ball), using floured hands. Place 1½ inches apart on 2 lightly buttered baking sheets. Cover and let rise in a warm place (80° to 85°), free from drafts, 1 hour or until doubled in bulk.

5. Preheat oven to 375°. Stir together blueberries and preserves. Combine ⅓ cup flour and next 2 ingredients with a pastry blender until crumbly. Press thumb into each dough ball, forming an indentation; fill each with 1 Tbsp. berry mixture. Sprinkle with flour mixture. Bake at 375° for 20 to 25 minutes or until golden.

***Mango Kolaches*:** Prepare as directed, substituting 2 cups chopped fresh mango for blueberries and ⅓ cup peach preserves for blueberry preserves.

BAKING SECRETS
from the Southern Living Test Kitchen

Don't overwork the dough. You can use a cookie scoop for easy portioning in Step 4, if desired.

SOUR CREAM POCKETBOOK ROLLS

Recipes are often richer in the South, and the secret to the tender texture of these folded rolls is an entire container of sour cream. It imparts the subtle tang and moistness that makes these fluffy rolls perfect for accompanying a fancy roast or steaks.

makes about 4½ dozen rolls   hands-on 30 min.   total 9 hours, 32 min.

1 (8-oz.) container sour cream
½ cup butter
½ cup sugar
1¼ tsp. table salt
2 (¼-oz.) envelopes active dry yeast

½ cup warm water (100° to 110°)
2 large eggs, lightly beaten
4 cups all-purpose flour
¼ cup butter, melted and divided

1. Cook first 4 ingredients in a saucepan over medium-low heat, stirring occasionally, 3 to 4 minutes or until butter melts. Let cool to 115°.

2. Combine yeast and warm water in a 1-cup liquid measuring cup; let stand 5 minutes. Stir together eggs, flour, yeast mixture, and sour cream mixture in a large bowl until well blended. Cover and chill 8 to 24 hours.

3. Divide dough into fourths, and shape each portion into a ball. Roll each ball to ¼-inch thickness on a floured surface; cut dough into rounds with a 2½-inch round cutter.

4. Brush rounds with 2 Tbsp. melted butter. Make a crease across each round with a knife, and fold in half; gently press edges to seal. Place rolls, with sides touching, in a lightly greased 15- x 10-inch jelly-roll pan. Place any remaining rolls on a lightly greased baking sheet. Cover and let rise in a warm place (80° to 85°), free from drafts, 45 minutes or until doubled in bulk.

5. Preheat oven to 375°. Bake rolls at 375° for 12 to 15 minutes or until golden brown. Brush rolls with remaining 2 Tbsp. melted butter.

ICEBOX DINNER ROLLS

*Also known as "cloverleaf rolls" because of their signature
triple-bump tops, these rolls are made by shaping three mini rolls
and nesting them all together in a greased muffin pan before baking.*

makes about 1½ dozen   hands-on 30 min.   total 9 hours, 35 min.

1   cup boiling water
6   Tbsp. shortening
¼   cup sugar
1   tsp. table salt
1   (¼-oz.) envelope active dry yeast

¼   cup warm water (100° to 110°)
1   large egg, lightly beaten
4   cups all-purpose flour
¼   cup butter, melted and divided

1. Pour boiling water over shortening and next 2 ingredients in bowl of a heavy-duty electric stand mixer, and stir until shortening melts and sugar and salt are completely dissolved. Let stand 10 minutes or until about 110°.

2. Meanwhile, combine yeast and warm water in a 1-cup liquid measuring cup; let stand 5 minutes.

3. Add yeast mixture and egg to shortening mixture; beat at low speed until combined. Gradually add flour, beating at low speed 2 to 3 minutes or until flour is blended and dough is soft and smooth.

4. Place dough in a lightly greased bowl, turning to grease top. Cover and chill 8 to 24 hours.

5. Turn dough out onto a lightly floured surface, and knead until smooth and elastic (about 1 minute). Gently shape dough into 60 (1-inch) balls; place 3 dough balls in each cup of 2 lightly greased 12-cup muffin pans. (You will fill only 20 cups.) Brush rolls with half of melted butter.

6. Cover pans with plastic wrap, and let rise in a warm place (80° to 85°), free from drafts, 45 minutes to 1 hour or until doubled in bulk.

7. Preheat oven to 400°. Bake rolls at 400° for 8 to 12 minutes or until golden brown. Brush with remaining melted butter. Serve immediately.

xxxxxxxxxxxxxxxxxxxxxxxxxxxxxxxxxxxxxxx

time-saving tip

If you can't start making these rolls a day ahead, accelerate
Step 4 by placing bowl of dough in a warm place, free of
drafts (80° to 85°), and letting rise until doubled, about 1½ to
2 hours. Continue with recipe as directed.

xxxxxxxxxxxxxxxxxxxxxxxxxxxxxxxxxxxxxxx

41

CARAMELIZED ONION AND SWISS POPOVERS

*A hot pan and oven temperature get popovers off to
a high-rising start, while lowering the temperature midway
through baking helps prevent an out-of-the-oven collapse.*

makes 8 popovers   hands-on 10 min.   total 1 hour, 35 min., including onions

1   cup all-purpose flour
1   cup 2% reduced-fat milk,
    at room temperature
3   large eggs, at room temperature
2   Tbsp. butter, melted
¾   tsp. table salt

¼   cup (1 oz.) freshly shredded
    Swiss cheese
¼   cup Caramelized Sweet Onions, chopped
1   Tbsp. chopped fresh chives
4   tsp. canola oil

1. Preheat oven to 425°. Heat a 12-cup muffin pan in oven 10 minutes.

2. Meanwhile, process first 5 ingredients in a blender or food processor 20 to 30 seconds or until smooth. Stir in cheese and next 2 ingredients.

3. Remove pan from oven; pour ½ tsp. oil into each of 8 muffin cups, filling center 6 cups and middle cup on each end. Heat in oven 5 minutes. Remove from oven. Divide batter among oiled muffin cups; return to oven immediately.

4. Bake at 425° for 15 to 20 minutes or until puffed and lightly browned around edges. Reduce oven temperature to 350°; bake 10 minutes or until tops are golden brown.

5. Transfer to a wire rack; cool 3 to 4 minutes before serving.

CARAMELIZED SWEET ONIONS

*The trick is to cook the onions slowly, allowing the natural sugars
to caramelize. Make several batches, and store in freezer.*

12   cups sliced sweet onions (about 2½ lb.)   1   tsp. table salt

Heat a large nonstick skillet over medium heat. Add sweet onions, and cook, stirring often, 30 minutes or until onions are caramel colored, sprinkling with salt halfway through. **Makes about 3 cups.**

Note: Store in refrigerator in an airtight container or a zip-top plastic freezer bag up to 1 week, or freeze up to 2 months.

Sally Lunn

Sorghum-Oat
Bread

Country Crust
Bread

Pumpernickel
Bread

SORGHUM~OAT BREAD

(pictured on page 44)

*With distinctive sweetness from sorghum syrup—the sweetener long revered in the
Appalachian mountains of the South—and brown sugar plus a hint of cinnamon spice,
these impressive loaves look and taste like they came right from a country bakery.*

makes 2 loaves   hands-on 25 min.   total 4 hours, 20 min.

2¼	cups boiling water	1	Tbsp. active dry yeast
1	cup uncooked regular oats	1	tsp. granulated sugar
¼	cup butter	4	cups bread flour
½	cup firmly packed dark brown sugar	1½	cups whole wheat flour
2	Tbsp. sorghum syrup	1	Tbsp. table salt
1	Tbsp. fresh lemon juice	1	tsp. ground cinnamon
½	cup warm water (100° to 110°)	2	Tbsp. butter, melted

1. Stir together first 3 ingredients in bowl of a heavy-duty electric stand mixer until butter
melts. Stir in brown sugar and next 2 ingredients. Cool until lukewarm (20 to 30 minutes).

2. Meanwhile, stir together ½ cup warm water, yeast, and granulated sugar in a 1-cup glass
measuring cup; let stand 5 minutes.

3. Stir together bread flour and next 3 ingredients in a medium bowl. Stir yeast mixture
into oat mixture. Gradually add flour mixture to oat mixture, beating on low speed until
well blended.

4. Turn dough out onto a heavily floured surface with bread flour, and knead until smooth
and elastic (about 6 to 8 minutes), sprinkling surface with bread flour as needed. Place dough
in a lightly greased large bowl, turning to grease top. Cover and let rise in a warm place
(80° to 85°), free from drafts, about 1 hour or until doubled in bulk.

5. Punch dough down; turn out onto a lightly floured surface. Divide dough in half. Roll
each half into an 18- x 9-inch rectangle. Starting at short end, tightly roll up each rectangle,
jelly-roll fashion, pressing to seal edges as you roll. Pinch ends of dough to seal, and tuck ends
under dough. Place each dough roll, seam side down, in a lightly greased 9- x 5-inch loaf pan.
Cover and let rise in a warm place (80° to 85°), free from drafts, 1 hour or until doubled in bulk.

6. Preheat oven to 350°. Bake at 350° for 30 to 35 minutes or until loaves are golden brown and
sound hollow when tapped. Remove from pans to a wire rack, and brush loaves with melted
butter. Cool completely (about 1 hour).

SALLY LUNN

(pictured on page 44)

This no-knead recipe came from England, but Southerners have been starry-eyed for the brioche-like loaf for decades. This semisweet bread has the perfect texture for French toast, bread pudding, or toast with jam.

makes 8 to 10 servings   hands-on 15 min.   total 2 hours

1   cup warm milk (100° to 110°)
1   (¼-oz.) envelope active dry yeast
1   tsp. sugar
4   cups all-purpose flour
¼   to ½ cup sugar

1   tsp. table salt
3   large eggs, lightly beaten
½   cup warm water (100° to 110°)
½   tsp. baking soda
½   cup butter, melted

1. Stir together first 3 ingredients in a 2-cup glass measuring cup; let stand 5 minutes.

2. Stir together flour and next 2 ingredients in a large bowl. Stir in eggs until well blended. (Dough will look shaggy.) Stir together warm water and baking soda. Stir yeast mixture, soda mixture, and melted butter into flour mixture until well blended.

3. Spoon batter into a well-greased 10-inch (14-cup) tube pan. Cover with plastic wrap, and let rise in a warm place (80° to 85°), free from drafts, 45 minutes to 1 hour or until doubled in bulk.

4. Preheat oven to 400°. Carefully place pan in oven. (Do not agitate dough.) Bake at 400° for 25 to 30 minutes or until a wooden pick inserted in center comes out clean. Remove from pan to a wire rack, and cool 30 minutes before slicing.

BAKING SECRETS
from the Southern Living Test Kitchen

There are two main kinds of yeast breads, kneaded and batter. In kneaded yeast breads, the dough must be worked by hand or machine to develop the gluten. The kneading process gives the bread a finer texture, while the sticky batter bread dough has a coarser texture after baking.

COUNTRY CRUST BREAD

(*pictured on page 45*)

This top-rated bread has a tender crumb and a soft crust that's very similar to sliced white bread that you can find at the grocery store, yet far more delicious.

makes 2 loaves   hands-on 25 min.   total 3 hours, 50 min.

2	(¼-oz.) envelopes active dry yeast	1	Tbsp. table salt
2	cups warm water (100° to 110°)	1	Tbsp. lemon juice
½	cup sugar	6	to 6½ cups bread flour
2	large eggs	1	Tbsp. vegetable oil
¼	cup vegetable oil	1½	Tbsp. butter, melted

1. Combine yeast, warm water, and 2 tsp. sugar in bowl of a heavy-duty electric stand mixer; let stand 5 minutes. Stir in eggs, next 3 ingredients, 3 cups flour, and remaining sugar. Beat dough at medium speed, using paddle attachment, until smooth. Gradually beat in remaining 3 to 3½ cups flour until a soft dough forms.

2. Turn dough out onto a heavily floured surface, and knead until smooth and elastic (about 8 to 10 minutes), sprinkling surface with flour as needed. Place dough in a lightly greased large bowl, turning to grease top. Cover and let rise in a warm place (80° to 85°), free from drafts, about 1 hour or until doubled in bulk.

3. Punch dough down; turn out onto a lightly floured surface. Divide dough in half.

4. Roll each dough half into an 18- x 9-inch rectangle. Starting at 1 short end, tightly roll up each rectangle, jelly-roll fashion, pressing to seal edges as you roll. Pinch ends of dough to seal, and tuck ends under dough. Place each dough roll, seam side down, in a lightly greased 9- x 5-inch loaf pan. Brush tops with oil. Cover and let rise in a warm place (80° to 85°), free from drafts, 1 hour or until doubled in bulk.

5. Preheat oven to 375°. Bake at 375° for 25 to 30 minutes or until loaves are deep golden brown and sound hollow when tapped. Remove from pans to a wire rack, and brush loaves with melted butter. Let cool completely (about 1 hour).

Country Crust Wheat Bread: Substitute 3 cups wheat flour for 3 cups bread flour.

Country Crust Cheese Bread: Sprinkle 1 cup (4 oz.) freshly shredded sharp Cheddar cheese onto each dough rectangle before rolling up.

PUMPERNICKEL BREAD

(pictured on page 45)

*For perfect pumpernickel bread that's hearty with just a touch of sweetness,
use bread flour and rye flour, and add molasses and instant coffee granules for flavor.*

makes 1 loaf   hands-on 20 min.   total 1 hour, 20 min.

1¾ cups warm water (100° to 110°)
1   (¼-oz.) envelope active dry yeast
2   Tbsp. sugar
2   Tbsp. instant coffee granules
¼   cup molasses
4½ cups bread flour

1   cup rye flour
2   tsp. table salt
Parchment paper
Vegetable cooking spray
2   Tbsp. butter, melted

1. Preheat oven to 200°. Stir together first 3 ingredients in bowl of a heavy-duty electric stand mixer. Let stand 5 minutes.

2. Add coffee and next 4 ingredients to yeast mixture. Beat at low speed, using dough hook attachment, for 1 minute or until soft dough comes together. Beat at medium speed 4 minutes. (Dough will be slightly sticky.)

3. Turn dough out onto a lightly floured surface; shape dough into a 9- x 5-inch oval loaf. Place on a parchment paper-lined baking sheet; coat lightly with cooking spray, and cover loosely with plastic wrap. Turn oven off, and place loaf in oven. Let rise 30 minutes or until loaf is doubled in bulk. Remove loaf from oven. Remove and discard plastic wrap.

4. Preheat oven to 375°. Bake bread at 375° for 30 to 35 minutes. Remove from oven, and brush with melted butter. Cool on wire rack.

German-Style Pumpernickel Rolls: Pat dough into a 10-inch square (½ inch thick). Cut into 2-inch squares. Roll into 1½-inch balls, and place on a parchment paper-lined baking sheet. Proceed with recipe as directed. Bake at 375° for 10 to 12 minutes or until lightly browned.

German-Style Pumpernickel Rolls with Caraway: Follow instructions for German-Style Pumpernickel Rolls, adding 1 Tbsp. caraway seeds. Proceed with recipe as directed.

Walnut-Raisin Pumpernickel Boule: Add ¾ cup raisins (or golden raisins) and 1 cup coarsely chopped toasted walnuts to dough before mixing. Shape dough into a ball, and gently flatten into a 7-inch circle. Cut 3 slits in dough (¼ to ½ inch deep) with a sharp paring knife just before baking, if desired. Whisk together 1 egg white and 3 Tbsp. water in a small bowl; brush loaf with egg mixture. Bake at 375° for 38 minutes or until a wooden pick inserted in center comes out clean. Omit brushing on melted butter.

BRAIDED EGG BREAD

This slightly sweet bread is also known as challah (pronounced KHAH-lah). It's delicious for French toast.

makes 2 loaves   hands-on 30 min.   total 1 hour, 50 min.

1½ cups milk	1 large egg yolk
2 (¼-oz.) packages active dry yeast	½ cup honey
5½ cups all-purpose flour	All-purpose flour
1 tsp. table salt	Parchment paper
¼ cup shortening	1 large egg, lightly beaten
3 large eggs	1 tsp. sesame seeds (optional)

1. Preheat oven to 200°. Microwave 1½ cups milk in a microwave-safe glass bowl at HIGH 2 to 3 minutes or until heated. Stir in yeast; let stand 5 minutes.

2. Combine 5½ cups flour and salt in a large bowl; stir in yeast mixture. Add shortening and next 3 ingredients. Beat at low speed with an electric mixer 1 to 2 minutes. Beat at medium speed 5 more minutes.

3. Sprinkle dough with additional flour, and remove from bowl. (Dough will be very sticky.) Place dough in a lightly greased bowl, turning to grease top. Turn off oven. Cover bowl with plastic wrap, and let rise in oven 30 minutes or until doubled in bulk. Remove from oven. Remove and discard plastic wrap.

4. Punch dough down, and divide in half. Divide each half into 3 equal portions. Roll each portion into a 14-inch-long rope; pinch 3 ropes together at 1 end to seal, and braid. Repeat with remaining dough portions. Place braids on a parchment paper-lined baking sheet.

5. Preheat oven to 350°. Cover braids with plastic wrap, and let rise in a warm place (80° to 85°), free from drafts, 25 to 30 minutes or until doubled in bulk. Brush evenly with beaten egg, and sprinkle with sesame seeds, if desired.

6. Bake at 350° for 25 minutes or until golden. (A wooden pick inserted in center should come out clean.)

HONEY~OATMEAL WHEAT BREAD

Honey and molasses give this whole-grain bread a gentle sweetness, while molasses also imparts a deep brown color.

makes 2 loaves or 24 servings   hands-on 25 min.   total 3 hours

2   cups warm water (100° to 110°)
3   Tbsp. molasses
1   (¼-oz.) envelope active dry yeast
3   cups all-purpose flour, divided
2½ cups whole wheat flour
1   cup uncooked regular oats, plus more for sprinkling

1   Tbsp. table salt
¼   cup honey
3   Tbsp. olive oil
6   Tbsp. all-purpose flour
Vegetable cooking spray

1. Combine first 3 ingredients in a 2-cup glass measuring cup; let yeast mixture stand 5 minutes. Combine 2 cups all-purpose flour, whole wheat flour, oats, and salt.

2. Beat yeast mixture, 1 cup all-purpose flour, honey, and olive oil at medium speed with a heavy-duty electric stand mixer until well blended. Gradually add whole wheat flour mixture, beating at low speed until a soft dough forms.

3. Turn dough out onto a heavily floured surface, and knead 9 minutes, adding additional all-purpose flour (up to 6 Tbsp.) as needed. (Dough will be slightly sticky.) Place dough in a large bowl coated with cooking spray, turning to grease dough. Cover bowl with plastic wrap, and let rise in a warm place (80° to 85°), free from drafts, 1 hour or until doubled in bulk.

4. Punch dough down, and divide in half. Roll each portion into a 13- x 8-inch rectangle on a lightly floured surface. Roll up each dough rectangle, jelly-roll fashion, starting at 1 short side; pinch ends to seal. Place loaves, seam sides down, into 2 (8½- x 4½-inch) loaf pans coated with cooking spray. Cover loosely with plastic wrap, and let rise in a warm place (80° to 85°), free from drafts, 45 minutes or until almost doubled in bulk. Remove and discard plastic wrap. Sprinkle loaves with additional oats.

5. Preheat oven to 350°. Bake at 350° for 30 to 35 minutes or until loaves sound hollow when tapped and are golden. Cool in pans on wire racks 10 minutes. Remove loaves from pans, and cool on wire racks.

✕✕✕✕✕✕✕✕✕✕✕✕✕✕✕✕✕✕✕✕✕✕✕✕✕✕✕✕✕✕✕✕✕

time-saving tip

This recipe makes two loaves, so freeze one after cooling to help it stay fresh longer. Slice first, if desired; then wrap the loaf in plastic wrap and aluminum foil, and place in a zip-top plastic freezer bag. Keep frozen for up to 1 month.

✕✕✕✕✕✕✕✕✕✕✕✕✕✕✕✕✕✕✕✕✕✕✕✕✕✕✕✕✕✕✕✕✕

FIGGY FOCACCIA

When figs are ripe, there are never too many ways to incorporate them into every meal. Combined with red onions and fresh rosemary, figs are the star topping in this chewy bread that is similar to a pizza.

makes 4 to 6 servings   hands-on 20 min.   total 35 min.

1   medium-size red onion
3   Tbsp. olive oil, divided
Coarse sea or kosher salt and freshly
    ground black pepper to taste

Plain white cornmeal
1   lb. bakery pizza dough
8   fresh figs, halved
1   Tbsp. fresh rosemary leaves

1. Preheat grill to 350° to 400° (medium-high) heat. Cut onion into ¾- to 1-inch slices. Brush onion slices with 1 Tbsp. olive oil, and season with sea salt and freshly ground pepper to taste. Grill onion slices, without grill lid, 3 to 4 minutes on each side or until tender and lightly charred.

2. Preheat oven to 425°. Lightly dust work surface with cornmeal. Stretch dough into a 10- to 12-inch oval on work surface. Place dough, cornmeal side down, on a greased baking sheet; drizzle with remaining 2 Tbsp. olive oil. Rub oil into dough. Arrange fig halves and grilled onion over dough, pressing lightly. Sprinkle with rosemary and salt and pepper to taste.

3. Bake at 425° on lowest oven rack 15 to 20 minutes or until golden.

XXXXXXXXXXXXXXXXXXXXXXXXXXXXXXXX

sweet idea

Turn this into a pizza by adding grated
fontina cheese and sliced dry salami.

XXXXXXXXXXXXXXXXXXXXXXXXXXXXXXXX

ROSEMARY FOCACCIA BREAD

This bread gets its signature look from the small indentations made with a wooden spoon all across the soft dough before baking. Once baked, the web-like holes throughout are perfect for soaking up olive oil or pasta sauce.

makes 10 to 12 servings   hands-on 30 min.   total 3 hours

1	(¼-oz.) envelope active dry yeast	1	Tbsp. table salt
1⅔	cups warm water (100° to 110°)	2	Tbsp. fresh rosemary leaves, divided
4½	cups bread flour	3	Tbsp. extra virgin olive oil
¼	cup extra virgin olive oil	1	tsp. kosher salt

1. Stir together yeast and warm water in bowl of a heavy-duty electric stand mixer; let stand 5 minutes.

2. Add bread flour, ¼ cup oil, and 1 Tbsp. table salt to yeast mixture. Beat on low speed, using paddle attachment, 10 seconds or until blended. Increase speed to medium. Beat 45 seconds or until dough is smooth. Add 1 Tbsp. rosemary. Replace paddle attachment with dough hook; increase speed to medium-high, and beat 4 minutes. (Dough will be sticky.)

3. Turn out dough onto a floured surface, and knead until smooth and elastic (about 1 minute). Place in a greased bowl, turning to coat. Cover dough with plastic wrap, and let rise in a warm place (80° to 85°), free from drafts, 1 hour or until doubled in bulk.

4. Press dough into a well greased 15- x 10-inch jelly-roll pan, pressing to about ¼-inch thickness. Cover with a kitchen towel, and let rise in a warm place 1 hour.

5. Preheat oven to 475°. Press handle of a wooden spoon into dough to make indentations at 1-inch intervals; drizzle with 3 Tbsp. oil. Sprinkle with kosher salt and remaining 1 Tbsp. rosemary. Bake at 475° for 14 to 16 minutes or until top is light brown. Remove from pan to a wire rack, and cool 10 minutes.

xxxxxxxxxxxxxxxxxxxxxxxxxxxxxxxxxxxxxx

sweet idea

Serve this bread, warm from the oven, as an appetizer alongside a fruity, extra-virgin olive oil for dipping.

xxxxxxxxxxxxxxxxxxxxxxxxxxxxxxxxxxxxxx

biscuits
& cornbread

BISCUITS & CORNBREAD

Whether making flaky, feather-light biscuits or a skillet full of cornbread,
it's easy to whip up the perfect batch of these Southern staples.

Follow along as we show you our tips and tricks for the ultimate buttermilk biscuit and the perfect wedge of cornbread. Even if you've been baking for years, sometimes even the simplest change in technique can vastly improve the finished product. Serve them for breakfast on Saturday morning or bring a basketful to the family reunion. Our classic recipes throughout this chapter are sure to win over any crowd.

......making biscuits......

Step 1: Grate frozen butter. It's our favorite fast-and-easy technique to incorporate ice-cold fat into flour.

Step 2: Stir together all ingredients exactly 15 times to form a ragged, sticky dough.

Step 3: For drop biscuits, scoop dough onto a parchment-lined baking sheet, at least an inch apart. (Use a 2-inch cookie scoop.)

Step 4: For rolled and cut biscuits, fold and roll the dough 5 times before cutting. This creates buttery layers that bake up flaky.

Step 5: Punch straight down when cutting. Don't twist; it will ruin your layers and reduce the overall rise.

Step 6: Arrange dough rounds so the sides touch. The biscuits will help each other rise to the occasion.

Step 7: Bake at 475° for 12 to 15 minutes or until lightly browned. Brush with melted butter.

Step 8: To split a biscuit, gently spear the biscuit all the way around with the tines of a fork (as you would do with an English muffin). Carefully pull biscuit into halves.

......making cornbread.......

Step 1: Preheat oven and place bacon drippings in a cast-iron skillet; heat in oven 8 to 10 minutes or until drippings begin to gently smoke.

Step 2: Meanwhile, stir together cornmeal and other dry ingredients in a large bowl.

Step 3: Stir together liquid ingredients, including eggs, in a medium bowl.

Step 4: During the last minute the skillet is heating in oven, stir liquid mixture into cornmeal mixture until just combined.

Step 5: Pour hot drippings into cornmeal mixture, and quickly stir to blend.

Step 6: Pour mixture into hot skillet, and immediately place in hot oven.

Step 7: Bake until golden brown and cornbread releases from sides of skillet or a toothpick inserted into center comes out clean. Cool 1 to 2 minutes.

Step 8: To turn out cornbread, place serving platter on top of skillet. Hold skillet handle with oven mitt and place other hand on platter.

Step 9: Carefully invert skillet to release cornbread onto a platter.

Step 10: Set hot skillet aside and carefully flip cornbread right side up.

Step 11: Slice cornbread into wedges to serve immediately, or cool completely and wrap tightly to serve later.

HUSH PUPPIES

While many might argue over the origination of the name "hush puppy," there's no denying that even the simplest version of these mini cornbread bites can be the perfect sidekick for just about any Southern fry-up.

makes about 2½ dozen hush puppies   hands-on 20 min.   total 20 min.

Vegetable oil
1   cup self-rising yellow cornmeal mix
½   cup self-rising flour
1   tsp. sugar

½   tsp. baking soda
1   cup diced onion
¾   cup buttermilk

1. Pour oil to depth of 2 inches into a Dutch oven; heat to 375°. Stir together cornmeal and next 4 ingredients in a large bowl. Add buttermilk, stirring just until moistened. (Mixture will be slightly thicker than cake batter.)

2. Drop batter by teaspoonfuls into hot oil, and fry, in batches, 2 to 3 minutes or until golden brown, turning often. Drain on a wire rack over paper towels; serve immediately.

BAKING SECRETS
from the Southern Living Test Kitchen

The oil for frying hush puppies should be 2 to 3 inches deep and heated until very hot, about 375°.
Fry only a few at a time so the oil doesn't cool down; you want them to be crisp and golden.

SKILLET CORNBREAD

Quickly incorporate the hot bacon drippings into the batter with
a fork. When you pour it back into the hot skillet, listen for the sizzle.
That sound means your crust will be dark golden and crisp.

makes 6 to 8 servings   hands-on 20 min.   total 40 min.

2	Tbsp. bacon drippings	1	tsp. baking soda
1½	cups stone-ground white cornmeal	¾	tsp. table salt
¼	cup all-purpose flour	2	cups buttermilk
2	tsp. sugar	1	large egg
1	tsp. baking powder		

1. Preheat oven to 450°. Place bacon drippings in a 10-inch cast-iron skillet, and heat in oven 8 to 10 minutes or until drippings begin to gently smoke.

2. Meanwhile, stir together cornmeal and next 5 ingredients in a large bowl. Stir together buttermilk and egg in a medium bowl.

3. During last minute skillet is heating in oven, stir buttermilk mixture into cornmeal mixture until just combined. Pour hot drippings into cornmeal mixture, and quickly stir to blend. Pour mixture into hot skillet, and immediately place in oven.

4. Bake at 450° for 18 to 20 minutes or until golden brown and cornbread pulls away from sides of skillet. Remove from skillet, and serve immediately.

Griddle Cakes: Place bacon drippings in skillet, and heat over medium-high heat 2 to 3 minutes or until drippings begin to gently smoke. Add 1 cup fresh corn kernels and ¼ cup finely chopped sweet onion to drippings, and sauté 3 to 4 minutes or until lightly charred. Stir together cornmeal and next 7 ingredients in a large bowl. Stir in corn mixture. Pour about 2 Tbsp. batter for each griddle cake onto a hot, buttered griddle or into a large nonstick skillet. Cook 2 to 3 minutes or until tops are covered with bubbles and edges look dry and cooked. Turn and cook 2 to 3 minutes or until golden brown. Place in a single layer on a baking sheet, and keep warm in a 200° oven up to 30 minutes.

xxxxxxxxxxxxxxxxxxxxxxxxxxxxxxxxxxxxx

sweet idea

Alongside an ample amount of softened butter, be sure
to provide your guests with a dish of honey
so they can sweeten up their wedge of cornbread.

xxxxxxxxxxxxxxxxxxxxxxxxxxxxxxxxxxxxx

SWEET POTATO CORNBREAD

Sandwich your favorite barbecue between slices of Sweet Potato Cornbread for a change of pace, or serve alongside your favorite meal as you would regular cornbread. The sweet potatoes add a touch of sweetness to this favorite bread of the South.

makes 6 servings   hands-on 15 min.   total 50 min.

2   cups self-rising white cornmeal mix
3   Tbsp. sugar
¼   tsp. pumpkin pie spice
5   large eggs

2   cups mashed cooked sweet potatoes (about 1½ lb. sweet potatoes)
1   (8-oz.) container sour cream
½   cup butter, melted

1. Preheat oven to 425°. Stir together first 3 ingredients in a large bowl; make a well in center of mixture. Whisk together eggs and next 3 ingredients; add to cornmeal mixture, stirring just until moistened. Spoon batter into a lightly greased 9-inch square pan.

2. Bake at 425° for 35 minutes or until golden brown.

~ BAKING SECRETS ~
from the Southern Living Test Kitchen

Cook whole, unpeeled sweet potatoes by boiling them in water for 30 minutes. Once fork-tender, submerge them in cold water; the peels will be very easy to remove.

Grannie's Cracklin' Cornbread

Cornbread Madeleines

Cornbread Focaccia

Lace Cornbread

GRANNIE'S CRACKLIN' CORNBREAD

(pictured on page 68)

*True cracklings in this traditional Southern cornbread are crispy pieces
of pork or poultry fat after they have been rendered, or the crisp,
brown skin of fried or roasted pork. Bacon makes a fine substitute.*

makes 8 to 10 servings   hands-on 10 min.   total 39 min.

¼   cup butter
2   cups self-rising yellow cornmeal mix
½   cup all-purpose flour

2½   cups buttermilk
2   large eggs, lightly beaten
1   cup cracklings*

1. Preheat oven to 425°. Place butter in a 9-inch cast-iron skillet, and heat in oven 4 minutes.

2. Combine cornmeal and flour in a large bowl; make a well in center of mixture.

3. Stir together buttermilk, eggs, and cracklings; add to dry ingredients, stirring just until moistened. Pour over melted butter in hot skillet.

4. Bake at 425° for 25 to 30 minutes or until golden brown.

* 1 cup cooked, crumbled bacon (12 to 15 slices) may be substituted for cracklings.

Grannie's Cracklin' Cakes: Prepare batter as directed above; stir in ¼ cup butter, melted. Heat a large skillet coated with vegetable cooking spray over medium-high heat. Spoon about ¼ cup batter for each cake into skillet; cook, in batches, 2 to 3 minutes on each side or until golden.

BAKING SECRETS
from the Southern Living Test Kitchen

Cornbread batter should be fairly thin and pourable.
If it seems too thick, add a little more liquid. Pouring the
batter into a very hot skillet gives it a crispy exterior.

CORNBREAD MADELEINES

(pictured on page 68)

These gems, a twist on the traditional French sponge cake, are one of our favorite hostess gifts. Light and airy, and not too sweet, they'd have Proust swooning "Lawdamercy."

makes 4 dozen madeleines   hands-on 10 min.   total 1 hour, 14 min.

2   cups self-rising white cornmeal mix
½   cup all-purpose flour
¼   cup sugar

2   cups buttermilk
½   cup butter, melted
2   large eggs, lightly beaten

Preheat oven to 400°. Whisk together cornmeal mix, flour, and sugar in a large bowl. Add buttermilk, melted butter, and eggs. Whisk together just until blended. Spoon batter into lightly greased shiny madeleine pans, filling three-fourths full. Bake at 400°, in batches, 16 to 18 minutes or until golden brown. Remove from pans immediately. Serve hot, or cool completely on wire racks (about 20 minutes), and freeze in zip-top plastic freezer bags up to 1 month. To serve, arrange desired amount of madeleines on a baking sheet, and bake at 350° for 5 to 6 minutes or until thoroughly heated.

Note: The traditional shiny heavy-gauge, tinned steel madeleine pan, which makes one dozen 3- x 2-inch madeleines, yields the prettiest results. (Dark nonstick versions tend to overbrown.) To prevent overbrowning if you do use a dark nonstick madeleine pan, wrap the bottom of the pan with a sheet of heavy-duty aluminum foil, shiny side out.

Orange-Rosemary Madeleines: Prepare recipe as directed, adding 2 Tbsp. orange zest and 1½ Tbsp. finely chopped fresh rosemary to dry ingredients.

Lemon-Thyme Madeleines: Prepare recipe as directed, adding 1 Tbsp. lemon zest and 1 Tbsp. finely chopped fresh thyme to dry ingredients.

Spicy White Cheddar Madeleines: Reduce sugar to 2 Tbsp. Prepare recipe as directed, adding ¾ cup finely shredded white Cheddar cheese and ¼ tsp. ground red pepper to dry ingredients.

CORNBREAD FOCACCIA

(pictured on page 69)

*This Southern take on an Italian classic is packed with flavor—
not just from a rainbow of toppings, but also thanks to a sprinkling
of yeast in the batter that gives this cornbread a bread-like taste.*

makes 8 to 10 servings   hands-on 15 min.   total 45 min.

2   cups self-rising white cornmeal mix
2   cups buttermilk
½   cup all-purpose flour
1   (¼-oz.) envelope rapid-rise yeast
2   large eggs, lightly beaten
¼   cup butter, melted

2   Tbsp. sugar
1   cup crumbled feta cheese
1   cup coarsely chopped black olives
¾   cup grape tomatoes, cut in half
1   Tbsp. coarsely chopped fresh
    rosemary

Preheat oven to 375°. Heat a well-greased 12-inch cast-iron skillet in oven 5 minutes. Stir together cornmeal mix and next 6 ingredients just until moistened; pour into hot skillet. Sprinkle with feta cheese, olives, tomatoes, and rosemary. Bake at 375° for 30 minutes or until golden brown.

Herbed Cornbread Focaccia: Prepare recipe as directed, omitting black olives and grape tomatoes; stir 1 Tbsp. each chopped fresh basil and chopped fresh parsley

LACE CORNBREAD

(pictured on page 69)

This old Southern take on cornbread is a crisp, lacy brown wafer best enjoyed a few seconds after it leaves the skillet. The thin batter spatters and sputters the second it hits the hot pan—that's how the lace is formed. This pretty cornbread was popular in the early twentieth century. Southern kitchens had all the ingredients on hand, and the wafers were inexpensive to make. It's worth the patience to cook them one at a time.

makes 10 pieces   hands-on 1 hour, 5 min.   total 1 hour, 5 min.

½   cup stone-ground white cornmeal
¼   tsp. table salt

¼   cup bacon drippings

1. Combine cornmeal, salt, and ¾ cup plus 2 Tbsp. water in a small bowl.

2. Heat 1 heaping Tbsp. bacon drippings in a cast-iron skillet over medium-low heat. When drippings are shimmering (the sign that they're hot), very carefully add 2 Tbsp. batter to hot pan. Gently spread batter from center outward. (The batter will immediately look lacy and bubbly.) Cook 3 minutes or until edges are browned. Turn and cook 3 minutes. Transfer to a wire rack. Repeat procedure with remaining batter, adding more drippings to pan as needed.

XXXXXXXXXXXXXXXXXXXXXXXXXXXXXXXXXX

sweet idea

Serve these with soup for lunch, with greens at supper,
or with preserves as a sweet snack.

XXXXXXXXXXXXXXXXXXXXXXXXXXXXXXXXXX

CHEESY CORNBREAD

*A heavy helping of freshly shredded sharp Cheddar is the perfect way
to upgrade classic cornbread. Add in one chopped seeded jalapeño
and 2 Tbsp. chopped green onions if you prefer cornbread with a kick.*

makes 8 servings   hands-on 10 min.   total 35 min.

3   tsp. vegetable oil
2   cups buttermilk
1   large egg

2   cups shredded sharp Cheddar cheese
1¾   cups self-rising yellow cornmeal mix

Preheat oven to 450°. Coat bottom and sides of an 8-inch cast-iron skillet with vegetable oil;
heat in oven 5 minutes. Whisk together buttermilk, egg, cheese, and cornmeal. Pour into hot
skillet. Bake at 450° for 25 minutes.

BAKING SECRETS
from the Southern Living Test Kitchen

Pay close attention to whether cornmeal, self-rising cornmeal,
or self-rising cornmeal mix is called for in these recipes.
Plain cornmeal has no additives. Self-rising cornmeal has
leavening agents and salt blended in the correct proportions
to ensure that baked goods rise properly. Cornmeal mix is
self-rising cornmeal plus flour added to lighten baked goods.

OUR FAVORITE BUTTERMILK BISCUIT

*After baking hundreds of biscuits, our Test Kitchen landed
on this winning recipe for Our Favorite Buttermilk Biscuit.
This no-fail version will impress new cooks and old pros alike.*

makes 12 to 14 biscuits   hands-on 25 min.   total 50 min.

½   cup butter, frozen
2½ cups self-rising flour
1   cup chilled buttermilk

Parchment paper
2   Tbsp. butter, melted

1. Preheat oven to 475°. Grate frozen butter using large holes of a box grater. Toss together grated butter and flour in a medium bowl. Chill 10 minutes.

2. Make a well in center of mixture. Add buttermilk, and stir 15 times. Dough will be sticky.

3. Turn dough out onto a lightly floured surface. Lightly sprinkle flour over top of dough. Using a lightly floured rolling pin, roll dough into a ¾-inch-thick rectangle (about 9 x 5 inches). Fold dough in half so short ends meet. Repeat rolling and folding process 4 more times.

4. Roll dough to ½-inch thickness. Cut with a 2½-inch floured round cutter, reshaping scraps and flouring as needed.

5. Place dough rounds on a parchment paper-lined jelly-roll pan. Bake at 475° for 15 minutes or until lightly browned. Brush with melted butter.

BAKING SECRETS
from the Southern Living Test Kitchen

If you like biscuits with crusty sides, place them 1 inch apart on a baking sheet. If you prefer soft sides, arrange biscuits close together in a shallow baking dish or pan.

77

CRUNCHY~BOTTOMED BISCUITS

The bottoms of these biscuits will end up crunchy and golden brown and will provide a sturdy base that holds up to a smothering of sausage gravy.

makes 12 to 14 biscuits   hands-on 25 min.   total 50 min.

½ cup butter, frozen
2½ cups self-rising flour
1   cup chilled buttermilk

Additional butter
2   Tbsp. butter, melted

1. Preheat oven to 475°. Grate frozen butter using large holes of a box grater. Toss together grated butter and flour in a medium bowl. Chill 10 minutes.

2. Make a well in center of mixture. Add buttermilk, and stir 15 times. (Dough will be sticky.)

3. Turn dough out onto a lightly floured surface. Lightly sprinkle flour over top of dough. Using a lightly floured rolling pin, roll dough into a ¾-inch-thick rectangle (about 9 x 5 inches). Fold dough in half so short ends meet. Repeat rolling and folding process 4 more times.

4. Roll dough to ½-inch thickness. Cut with a 2½-inch floured round cutter, reshaping scraps and flouring as needed.

5. Warm a cast-iron skillet in the oven, and spread a bit of butter in the skillet before adding dough rounds. Place dough rounds in skillet. Bake at 475° for 15 minutes or until lightly browned. Brush with melted butter.

xxxxxxxxxxxxxxxxxxxxxxxxxxxxxxxxxxxxxx

time-saving tip

If you want to make biscuits ahead of time or you
have leftover biscuits, you can wrap them in foil,
place them in a zip-top plastic freezer bag, and freeze
for up to 3 months. To serve, thaw biscuits and
place in a 300° oven for several minutes until heated.

xxxxxxxxxxxxxxxxxxxxxxxxxxxxxxxxxxxxxx

CAT-HEAD BISCUITS

Cat-head biscuits are delightfully huge, crispy-on-the-outside, fluffy-on-the-inside homemade biscuits. The name comes from their colossal size, about that of a cat's head. They bake longer and at a lower temperature than their smaller cousins.

makes 8 biscuits   hands-on 15 min.   total 45 min.

5   Tbsp. warm bacon drippings
5   Tbsp. unsalted butter, melted
3½ cups self-rising soft-wheat flour

1⅓ cups buttermilk, at room temperature
Parchment paper
Garnish: kosher salt

1. Preheat oven to 375°. Stir together bacon drippings and butter.

2. Place flour in a large bowl. Stir in drippings mixture and buttermilk, stirring just until a dough forms.

3. Turn dough out onto a lightly floured surface. Knead twice. Divide dough into 8 equal portions. Pat each portion into a 3½-inch round biscuit (about ¾ inch thick). Arrange 2 inches apart on a parchment paper-lined baking sheet.

4. Bake at 375° for 30 minutes or until tops are very lightly browned. Serve biscuits immediately, sprinkled with kosher salt, if desired.

Note: We tested with White Lily Self-Rising Flour.

xxxxxxxxxxxxxxxxxxxxxxxxxxxxxxxxxxxx

sweet idea

If you don't have bacon drippings on hand, cook
a pound of bacon before you start this recipe, reserve
the drippings, and serve the bacon with the biscuits
and a generous helping of sawmill or tomato gravy.

xxxxxxxxxxxxxxxxxxxxxxxxxxxxxxxxxxxx

Cornmeal-Chive
Biscuits

Sweet Potato
Biscuits

Fluffy Cream
Cheese Biscuits

French Onion
Biscuits

CORNMEAL~CHIVE BISCUITS

(pictured on page 82)

These biscuits have a dense and crunchy texture thanks to just ½ cup of cornmeal mix. Chopped green chives give them a subtle fresh onion flavor as well as a bit of color.

makes about 2 dozen biscuits   hands-on 20 min.   total 45 min.

2   cups self-rising soft-wheat flour
½   cup self-rising yellow cornmeal mix
½   cup cold butter
⅓   cup chopped fresh chives

1¼   cups whole buttermilk
Parchment paper
2   Tbsp. melted butter

1. Preheat oven to 425°. Combine flour and cornmeal in a large bowl. Cut butter into ½-inch-thick slices. Sprinkle butter over flour mixture, and toss. Cut butter into flour mixture with pastry blender or fork until crumbly. Cover and chill 10 minutes. Stir in chives. Add buttermilk, stirring just until dry ingredients are moistened.

2. Turn dough out onto floured surface, and knead 3 or 4 times, gradually adding additional self-rising flour as needed. With floured hands, pat dough into a ¾-inch-thick rectangle (about 9 x 5 inches); dust top with flour. Fold dough over itself in 3 sections, starting with short end (as if folding a letter-size piece of paper). Repeat 2 more times, beginning with patting dough into a rectangle.

3. Pat dough to ½-inch thickness. Cut with a 2-inch round cutter, and place, side by side, on a parchment paper-lined or lightly greased jelly-roll pan. (Dough rounds should touch.)

4. Bake at 425° for 13 to 15 minutes or until lightly browned. Remove from oven; brush with 2 Tbsp. melted butter.

BAKING SECRETS
from the Southern Living Test Kitchen

Press straight down with a biscuit cutter or glass for higher rising biscuits. If you twist the cutter, you'll seal the edges of the dough and the biscuits won't bake as tall.

SWEET POTATO BISCUITS

(pictured on page 82)

*Cooked sweet potatoes make for a very moist and tender biscuit
with a slightly orange hue. Serve these biscuits alongside a holiday feast
or offer them as an upgrade to the classic breakfast spread.*

makes 3 dozen biscuits   hands-on 30 min.   total 1 hour, 20 min.

5   cups self-rising flour
1   Tbsp. sugar
1   tsp. kosher salt
1   cup cold butter, cut into small cubes
¼   cup cold shortening

2   cups buttermilk
1   cup mashed cooked sweet potato
Parchment paper
2   Tbsp. butter, melted

1. Preheat oven to 425°. Stir together first 3 ingredients in a large bowl. Cut butter cubes and shortening into flour mixture with pastry blender or fork until crumbly. Cover and chill 10 minutes.

2. Whisk together buttermilk and sweet potato. Add to flour mixture, stirring just until dry ingredients are moistened.

3. Turn dough out onto a lightly floured surface, and knead lightly 3 or 4 times. Pat or roll dough to ¾-inch thickness; cut with a 2-inch round cutter, reshaping scraps once. Place rounds on a parchment paper-lined baking sheet.

4. Bake at 425° for 18 to 20 minutes or until biscuits are golden brown. Remove from oven, and brush tops of biscuits with melted butter. Serve immediately.

xxxxxxxxxxxxxxxxxxxxxxxxxxxxxxxxxxxxxx

sweet idea

Serve these from-scratch biscuits warm
with butter, honey, and jam, along with two platters—
one with seared slices of country ham and pepper jelly
and another with deli ham and pimiento cheese.

xxxxxxxxxxxxxxxxxxxxxxxxxxxxxxxxxxxxxx

FLUFFY CREAM CHEESE BISCUITS

(pictured on page 83)

Even without time to rise, just one envelope of active dry yeast, along with baking powder and soda, gives these biscuits a bread-like flavor and a lighter-than-air texture.

makes about 18 biscuits   hands-on 15 min.   total 33 min.

1   (¼-oz.) envelope active dry yeast
¼   cup warm water (100° to 110°)
5   cups all-purpose flour
2   Tbsp. sugar
1   Tbsp. baking powder
1   tsp. baking soda
1   tsp. table salt

1   (8-oz.) package cold cream cheese, cut into pieces
½   cup cold butter, cut into pieces
1¼   cups buttermilk
Parchment paper
2   Tbsp. butter, melted

1. Preheat oven to 400°. Combine yeast and warm water in a small bowl; let stand 5 minutes.

2. Meanwhile, whisk together flour and next 4 ingredients in a large bowl; cut cream cheese and cold butter into flour mixture with pastry blender or fork until crumbly.

3. Combine yeast mixture and buttermilk, and add to flour mixture, stirring just until dry ingredients are moistened. Turn dough out onto a lightly floured surface, and knead lightly 6 to 8 times (about 30 seconds to 1 minute), sprinkling with up to ¼ cup additional flour as needed to prevent sticking.

4. Roll dough to ¾-inch thickness. Cut with a 2½-inch round cutter, rerolling scraps once. Arrange biscuits on 2 parchment paper-lined baking sheets.

5. Bake at 400° for 13 to 15 minutes or until golden brown. Brush with melted butter.

FRENCH ONION BISCUITS

(pictured on page 83)

This recipe is great for when you want lots of flavor but don't want to have to worry about a long list of ingredients. French onion dip does double duty here—intense caramelized onion flavor, plus a tender biscuit crumb thanks to its sour cream base.

makes 1 dozen biscuits   hands-on 5 min.   total 18 min.

1   (8-oz.) container French onion dip
¼   cup milk
1   Tbsp. finely chopped fresh parsley

2   cups all-purpose baking mix
1   Tbsp. butter, melted

1. Preheat oven to 450°. Whisk together first 3 ingredients until smooth. Stir in baking mix until well blended. Divide dough into 12 equal portions, and arrange on a lightly greased baking sheet. Brush tops of dough with melted butter.

2. Bake at 450° for 7 to 8 minutes or until lightly golden. Let stand 5 minutes before serving.

Note: We tested with Bisquick All-Purpose Baking Mix.

Ranch Biscuits: Substitute 1 (8-oz.) container Ranch dip for French onion dip. Prepare recipe as directed.

BAKING SECRETS
from the Southern Living Test Kitchen

Once the package of all-purpose baking mix is opened, transfer the mix to an airtight container, and store in a cool, dry place such as the pantry to ensure freshness.

~ buttermilk ~

Though buttermilk seems richer and creamier than
regular milk, it actually contains the same fat content
as the whole, low-fat, and nonfat milks from which
it is made. Originally it was the liquid that remained
after churning the butter. Today's commercial
buttermilk is made by adding lactic acid to pasteurized,
homogenized milk, causing it to thicken and sour.

CORNBREAD BISCUITS

A cross between the South's two most prized breads, cornbread and biscuits, creates a hearty treat that's perfect for a simple breakfast or an evening feast. The combination of cold butter and shortening ensures a tender crumb and a dough that's easy to work with.

makes about 15 biscuits   hands-on 30 min.   total 53 min.

3   cups self-rising soft-wheat flour
½   cup self-rising yellow cornmeal mix
¼   cup cold butter, cut into pieces
¼   cup shortening, cut into pieces

1½   cups buttermilk
1   tsp. yellow cornmeal
2   Tbsp. butter, melted

1. Preheat oven to 500°. Whisk together first 2 ingredients in a large bowl. Cut in cold butter and shortening with pastry blender until mixture resembles small peas and dough is crumbly. Cover and chill 10 minutes. Add buttermilk, stirring just until dry ingredients are moistened.

2. Turn dough out onto a heavily floured surface; knead 3 or 4 times. Pat dough into a ¾-inch-thick circle.

3. Cut dough with a well-floured 2½-inch round cutter, rerolling scraps as needed. Sprinkle cornmeal on ungreased baking sheets; place biscuits on baking sheets. Lightly brush tops with 2 Tbsp. melted butter.

4. Bake at 500° for 13 to 15 minutes or until golden brown.

Note: We tested with White Lily Self-Rising Flour.

BAKING SECRETS
from the Southern Living Test Kitchen

Add your own signature spin with a few teaspoons of your favorite fresh herb, such as rosemary, sage, or thyme. Top with a sprinkle of sea salt after brushing with butter for a savory flavor boost.

ANGEL BISCUITS

The addition of yeast guarantees heavenly, fluffy biscuits every time.

makes about 2 dozen biscuits   hands-on 15 min.   total 32 min.

1   (¼-oz.) envelope active dry yeast
¼   cup warm water (100° to 110°)
5   cups all-purpose flour
2   Tbsp. sugar
1   Tbsp. baking powder

1   tsp. baking soda
1   tsp. table salt
½   cup shortening, cut into pieces
½   cup cold butter, cut into pieces
1½ cups buttermilk

1. Preheat oven to 400°. Combine yeast and warm water in a 1-cup glass measuring cup; let stand 5 minutes.

2. Meanwhile, whisk together flour and next 4 ingredients in a large bowl; cut in shortening and butter with pastry blender until crumbly.

3. Combine yeast mixture and buttermilk, and add to flour mixture, stirring just until dry ingredients are moistened. Turn dough out onto a lightly floured surface, and knead about 1 minute.

4. Roll dough to ½-inch thickness. Cut with a 2-inch round cutter or into 2-inch squares. Place on 2 ungreased baking sheets.

5. Bake at 400° for 12 to 15 minutes or until golden.

Cinnamon-Raisin Angel Biscuits: Substitute ¼ cup firmly packed brown sugar for 2 Tbsp. sugar. Stir 1 cup baking raisins, 2 tsp. lemon zest, and 1 tsp. ground cinnamon into flour mixture in Step 2. Proceed with recipe as directed.

✕✕✕✕✕✕✕✕✕✕✕✕✕✕✕✕✕✕✕✕✕✕✕✕✕✕✕✕✕✕

Time-saving Tip

Prepare recipe as directed through Step 3. Shape dough
into a disk; store in a glass airtight container in refrigerator
up to 5 days. Let stand at room temperature 5 minutes.
Roll, cut, and bake as directed in Steps 4 and 5. Unbaked
biscuits may be frozen on a baking sheet, covered with
plastic wrap, 2 hours. Transfer frozen biscuits to a zip-top
plastic freezer bag, and freeze up to 1 month. Let stand
at room temperature 30 minutes before baking as directed.

✕✕✕✕✕✕✕✕✕✕✕✕✕✕✕✕✕✕✕✕✕✕✕✕✕✕✕✕✕✕

BEST-EVER SCONES

*When our Test Kitchen first baked this simple scone recipe, we thought
they were the best we had ever tasted. Never fearing too much
of a good thing, we created eight sweet and savory variations.*

makes 8 servings   hands-on 15 min.   total 33 min.

2   cups all-purpose flour
⅓   cup sugar
1   Tbsp. baking powder
½   tsp. table salt

½   cup cold butter, cut into ½-inch cubes
1   cup whipping cream, divided
Wax paper

1. Preheat oven to 450°. Stir together first 4 ingredients in a large bowl. Cut butter into flour mixture with a pastry blender until it resembles small peas and dough is crumbly. Freeze 5 minutes. Add ¾ cup plus 2 Tbsp. cream, stirring just until dry ingredients are moistened.

2. Turn dough out onto wax paper; gently press or pat dough into a 7-inch round (mixture will be crumbly). Cut round into 8 wedges. Place wedges 2 inches apart on a lightly greased baking sheet. Brush tops of wedges with remaining 2 Tbsp. cream just until moistened.

3. Bake at 450° for 13 to 15 minutes or until golden.

Chocolate-Cherry Scones: Stir in ¼ cup dried cherries, coarsely chopped, and 2 oz. coarsely chopped semisweet chocolate with the cream.

Cranberry-Pistachio Scones: Stir in ¼ cup sweetened dried cranberries and ¼ cup coarsely chopped roasted salted pistachios with the cream.

Brown Sugar-Pecan Scones: Substitute brown sugar for granulated sugar. Stir in ½ cup toasted chopped pecans with the cream.

Bacon, Cheddar, and Chive Scones: Omit sugar. Stir in ¾ cup (3 oz.) shredded sharp Cheddar cheese, ¼ cup finely chopped cooked bacon, 2 Tbsp. chopped fresh chives, and ½ tsp. freshly ground black pepper with the cream.

Ham-and-Swiss Scones: Omit sugar. Stir in ¾ cup (3 oz.) shredded Swiss cheese and ¾ cup finely chopped baked ham with the cream. Serve warm with Mustard Butter: Stir together ½ cup softened butter, 1 Tbsp. spicy brown mustard, and 1 Tbsp. minced sweet onion.

Pimiento Cheese Scones: Omit sugar. Stir in ¾ cup (3 oz.) shredded sharp Cheddar cheese and 3 Tbsp. finely chopped pimiento with the cream.

Rosemary, Pear, and Asiago Scones: Omit sugar. Stir in ¾ cup finely chopped fresh pear, ½ cup grated Asiago cheese, and 1 tsp. chopped fresh rosemary with the cream.

Bite-Size Scones: Pat dough into 2 (4-inch) rounds. Cut rounds into 8 wedges. Bake as directed for 12 to 13 minutes.

SWEET SHORTCAKES

The sugar lends the biscuits a subtle sweetness, and the extra
fat in heavy cream gives them a crumbly texture like shortbread.
They're the perfect base for shortcake desserts.

makes 12 to 14 shortcakes   hands-on 25 min.   total 50 min.

½   cup butter, frozen
2½ cups self-rising flour
2   Tbsp. sugar

1   cup chilled heavy cream
Parchment paper
2   Tbsp. butter, melted

1. Preheat oven to 475°. Grate frozen butter using large holes of a box grater. Toss together grated butter, flour, and sugar in a medium bowl. Chill 10 minutes.

2. Make a well in center of mixture. Add cream, and stir 15 times. (Dough will be sticky.)

3. Turn dough out onto a lightly floured surface. Lightly sprinkle flour over top of dough. Using a lightly floured rolling pin, roll dough into a ¾-inch-thick rectangle (about 9 x 5 inches). Fold dough in half so short ends meet. Repeat rolling and folding process 4 more times.

4. Roll dough to ½-inch thickness. Cut with a 2½-inch floured round cutter, reshaping scraps and flouring as needed.

5. Place dough rounds on a parchment paper-lined jelly-roll pan. Bake at 475° for 15 minutes or until lightly browned. Brush with melted butter.

xxxxxxxxxxxxxxxxxxxxxxxxxxxxxxxxx

sweet idea

For the classic Strawberry Shortcake, combine quartered
strawberries with a sprinkling of granulated sugar;
let macerate for 10 minutes. Split cooled biscuits and
pile sweetened strawberries on biscuit base, top with
sweetened whipped cream, and replace biscuit tops.

xxxxxxxxxxxxxxxxxxxxxxxxxxxxxxxxx

quick breads
& muffins

QUICK BREADS & MUFFINS

Quick breads, whether as loaves, muffins, or even mini loaves, are by far the easiest and fastest way to bake up bread for morning, noon, or night.

Unlike traditional breads that call for yeast and must rise 1, 2, or 3 times, muffins and quick breads rely on baking powder or baking soda as leavening. That's why it's all the more important to ensure that your baking powder or soda is fresh, or your baked goods will turn out like hockey pucks. Learn all of our helpful tips and tricks by following these step-by-step guides for baking muffins and quick breads with ease.

......making quick bread......

Step 1: Combine wet ingredients in the bowl of an electric mixer.

Step 2: Add the sugar, and beat to incorporate air into the batter.

Step 3: Add the dry ingredients, blending until just incorporated.

Step 4: Stir in additional ingredients, like mashed bananas, flavorings, or add-ins like chocolate chips or nuts.

......testing for doneness......

Step 1: To check muffins for doneness, look for golden brown domed tops that spring back when lightly pressed with a finger.

Step 2: To check quick breads for doneness, look for a browned domed crust. Lightly press center; if it springs back, it's baked all the way through.

Step 3: You can also check the doneness of quick breads by piercing the center with a toothpick; it should come out clean or with a few crumbs.

making muffins

Step 1: Measure ingredients carefully, using dry measuring cups for flour and sugar, and glass measuring cups for all liquids and syrups.

Step 2: Gently stir dry ingredients together in a medium bowl and make a well in the center.

Step 3: Combine liquid ingredients in a small bowl, and pour into the well of dry ingredients.

Step 4: Stir mixture just until combined, taking care not to overmix. (Some lumps remaining are fine.)

Step 5: If adding fruit to muffins, stir in about 1 Tbsp. of reserved flour to help them stay suspended in batter.

Step 6: Carefully fold floured fruit into batter, taking care not to crush the fruit.

Step 7: Once the fruit is just incorporated, stop stirring the batter. Any additional stirring can cause the muffins to have a tough, chewy texture.

Step 8: If using muffin liners, lightly grease the inside of the liners with cooking spray so they will easily release from the baked muffins.

Step 9: Divide batter evenly among cups, filling two-thirds full.

Step 10: If not using muffin liners, lightly grease baking pan with cooking spray. Use a cookie scoop to quickly fill pan.

Step 11: Bake muffins as directed in recipe until domed and golden.

LEMON MUFFINS

Just a simple tart icing is all you need to take these basic lemon muffins to the next level. Serve them at a brunch or as an afternoon pick-me-up.

makes 1 dozen muffins   hands-on 10 min.   total 35 min.

3   cups all-purpose flour
1   cup sugar
2½   tsp. baking powder
½   tsp. table salt
2   large eggs

1¼   cups milk
½   cup butter, melted
1   Tbsp. firmly packed lemon zest
Lemon Icing

1. Preheat oven to 350°. Whisk together flour, sugar, baking powder, and salt in a large bowl.

2. Whisk together eggs, milk, melted butter, and lemon zest; stir into dry ingredients just until moistened. Spoon into a lightly greased 12-cup muffin pan, filling two-thirds full.

3. Bake at 350° for 25 to 30 minutes or until golden. Cool in pan on a wire rack 5 minutes. Remove from pan to wire rack, and cool completely (about 30 minutes).

4. Prepare Lemon Icing. Spoon icing over cooled muffins.

LEMON ICING

1   cup powdered sugar   1½   Tbsp. fresh lemon juice

Stir together powdered sugar and lemon juice in a small bowl until blended. Use immediately. **Makes about ½ cup.**

BAKING SECRETS
from the Southern Living Test Kitchen

One large lemon usually yields 2 to 3 Tbsp. juice and 2 tsp. zest. If you need zest, be sure to remove it from the lemon before squeezing the juice. To remove the zest, use a special zester or a fine grater. Once the zest is removed, refrigerate the remaining fruit up to a week.

BLACKBERRY CORNBREAD MUFFINS

With lots of fresh farm eggs, melted butter, and an entire container of sour cream, these muffins have a rich, pound cake-like texture. Studded with juicy, just-picked Southern blackberries, there's a burst of fruit in every bite.

makes 2 dozen muffins   hands-on 10 min.   total 1 hour

2	cups self-rising white cornmeal mix	1	(16-oz.) container sour cream
½	cup sugar	½	cup butter, melted
5	large eggs	2	cups fresh or frozen blackberries

1. Preheat oven to 450°. Stir together cornmeal mix and sugar in a large bowl; make a well in center of mixture. Whisk together eggs, sour cream, and butter; add to cornmeal mixture, stirring just until dry ingredients are moistened. Fold in blackberries. Spoon batter into 2 lightly greased 12-cup muffin pans, filling three-fourths full.

2. Bake at 450° for 15 to 17 minutes or until tops are golden brown. Cool in pans on a wire rack 5 minutes. Remove from pans to wire rack, and cool completely (about 30 minutes).

BAKING SECRETS
from the Southern Living Test Kitchen

Be careful not to overmix muffins. If you stir the batter until all the lumps are smooth, the muffins will be tough and have pointed tops. For tender muffins, stir the batter just enough to moisten the dry ingredients, and no more.

CARROT CAKE MUFFINS

Packed with pineapple, pecans, and raisins, as well as carrots, these loaded muffins are delicious and satisfying. If you're craving the sweetness of a classic carrot cake, just drizzle them with the Lemon-Cream Cheese Glaze found on page 114.

makes about 15 muffins   hands-on 20 min.   total 52 min.

Vegetable cooking spray
2   cups all-purpose flour
¾   cup granulated sugar
2   tsp. baking soda
1   tsp. ground cinnamon
1   tsp. table salt
1   (8-oz.) can crushed pineapple, drained

¼   cup vegetable oil
2   large eggs
2   large egg whites
1   Tbsp. vanilla extract
3   cups grated carrots
½   cup toasted chopped pecans
½   cup golden raisins

1. Preheat oven to 350°. Place about 15 paper baking cups in muffin pans, and coat with cooking spray.

2. Combine flour and next 4 ingredients in a large bowl; make a well in center of mixture. Whisk together pineapple and next 4 ingredients; add pineapple mixture to flour mixture, stirring just until dry ingredients are moistened. Fold in carrots, pecans, and raisins. Spoon batter into baking cups, filling about two-thirds full.

3. Bake at 350° for 22 to 25 minutes or until a wooden pick inserted in center comes out clean. Cool in pans on a wire rack 10 minutes. Serve warm or at room temperature.

xxxxxxxxxxxxxxxxxxxxxxxxxxxxxxxx

time-saving tip

Feel free to make these a day ahead so they're ready
to serve without any hassle. They will keep up to 3 days
stored at room temperature in a plastic bag, or freeze
them up to 3 months, wrapped in heavy-duty aluminum
foil and placed in a zip-top plastic freezer bag.

xxxxxxxxxxxxxxxxxxxxxxxxxxxxxxxxx

Strawberry-Lemonade
Muffins

Poppy Seed-Ginger
Muffins

Morning Glory
Muffins

Banana-Blueberry
Muffins

STRAWBERRY~ LEMONADE MUFFINS

(pictured on page 106)

With bright springtime flavor thanks to fresh berries and lemons, these muffins would be perfect for a light breakfast or as an addition to a brunch spread. Make these extra special by serving alongside store-bought or homemade lemon curd.

makes 15 muffins   hands-on 15 min.   total 42 min.

2½ cups self-rising flour
1¼ cups sugar, divided
1   (8-oz.) container sour cream
½   cup butter, melted

1   Tbsp. loosely packed lemon zest
¼   cup fresh lemon juice
2   large eggs, lightly beaten
1½ cups diced fresh strawberries

1. Preheat oven to 400°. Combine flour and 1 cup sugar in a large bowl; make a well in center of mixture.

2. Stir together sour cream and next 4 ingredients; add to flour mixture, stirring just until dry ingredients are moistened. Gently fold strawberries into batter. Spoon batter into lightly greased 12-cup muffin pans, filling three-fourths full. Sprinkle remaining ¼ cup sugar over batter.

3. Bake at 400° for 16 to 18 minutes or until golden brown and a wooden pick inserted in center comes out clean. Cool in pans on a wire rack 1 minute; remove from pans to wire rack, and cool 10 minutes.

BAKING SECRETS
from the Southern Living Test Kitchen

Be sure to take note that self-rising flour is called for in the recipe. However, you can substitute all-purpose flour with the following adjustments: For 1 cup self-rising flour, use 1 scant cup all-purpose flour plus 1 tsp. baking powder and ¼ tsp. table salt.

POPPY SEED~GINGER MUFFINS

(pictured on page 107)

*A sweet orange glaze is the perfect complement to these ginger muffins.
Add a little more orange juice if you prefer a thinner glaze,
or add a little more powdered sugar for a thicker consistency.*

makes 1½ dozen muffins   hands-on 15 min.   total 40 min.

¾   cup butter, softened
1⅓ cups sugar
2   large eggs, separated
3   cups cake flour
3½ tsp. baking powder
¼   tsp. table salt

1¼ cups milk
1   Tbsp. loosely packed orange zest
2   tsp. grated fresh ginger
2   tsp. vanilla extract
4   tsp. poppy seeds

1. Preheat oven to 350°. Beat butter at medium speed with a heavy-duty electric stand mixer until creamy. Gradually add sugar, beating until light and fluffy. Add egg yolks, 1 at a time, beating just until blended after each addition.

2. Stir together flour and next 2 ingredients. Stir together milk and next 3 ingredients. Add flour mixture to butter mixture alternately with milk mixture, beginning and ending with flour mixture. Beat at low speed just until blended after each addition. Beat egg whites until stiff peaks form; fold into batter. Stir in poppy seeds. Spoon into lightly greased 12-cup muffin pans, filling three-fourths full.

3. Bake at 350° for 18 to 20 minutes or until a wooden pick inserted in center comes out clean. Cool in pans on wire racks 5 minutes; transfer to wire racks.

ORANGE GLAZE

1½ cups powdered sugar   2   Tbsp. fresh orange juice

Stir together powdered sugar and orange juice. Drizzle over warm muffins. **Makes about ½ cup.**

BANANA~BLUEBERRY MUFFINS

(pictured on page 107)

Banana bread isn't your only option when bananas get extra ripe. Bake up these blueberry-studded muffins, made downright decadent with brown sugar and melted butter.

makes 1 dozen muffins   hands-on 12 min.   total 1 hour, 7 min.

1	cup fresh or frozen blueberries		1	cup mashed ripe banana
2	Tbsp. all-purpose flour		2	large eggs
2¼	cups all-purpose flour		¾	cup firmly packed light brown sugar
2	tsp. baking powder		⅓	cup butter, melted
½	tsp. ground cinnamon		½	tsp. vanilla extract
¼	tsp. table salt			

1. Preheat oven to 350°. Toss blueberries with 2 Tbsp. all-purpose flour. Stir together 2¼ cups all-purpose flour, baking powder, cinnamon, and salt.

2. Whisk together banana, eggs, brown sugar, melted butter, and vanilla; add to dry ingredients, stirring just until moistened. Fold in blueberries. Spoon into a lightly greased 12-cup muffin pan, filling two-thirds full.

3. Bake at 350° for 20 minutes or until golden brown. Cool in pan on a wire rack 5 minutes. Remove from pan to wire rack, and cool completely (about 30 minutes).

BAKING SECRETS
from the Southern Living Test Kitchen

If brown sugar becomes hard, microwave it at MEDIUM LOW (30% power) until softened, usually 1 to 2 minutes. Or, if you don't need the sugar right away, place an apple wedge in the bag, and seal overnight to soften.

MORNING GLORY MUFFINS

(pictured on page 107)

If you've ever taken a morning stroll in the South, you've surely noticed the white or blue trumpet-like flowers, for which these fruit-filled muffins are named, growing up fences, arbors, and mailbox posts. Whether freshly baked or made the night before, these baked goods will help you greet the day in full bloom.

makes 2 dozen muffins   hands-on 30 min.   total 1 hour, 28 min.

3 cups all-purpose flour	3 large eggs
1 tsp. table salt	2½ tsp. vanilla extract
1 tsp. baking soda	1 (8-oz.) can crushed pineapple, undrained
1 tsp. ground cinnamon	
½ tsp. ground nutmeg	2 large carrots, finely grated (1 cup)
2 cups sugar	1 cup toasted chopped pecans
¾ cup canola oil	1 cup golden raisins

1. Preheat oven to 350°. Combine flour, salt, baking soda, ground cinnamon, and nutmeg in a large bowl; make a well in center of mixture.

2. Whisk together sugar, canola oil, eggs, and vanilla; fold in crushed pineapple and carrots. Add to flour mixture, stirring just until dry ingredients are moistened. Fold in toasted pecans and raisins. Spoon into lightly greased muffin pans, filling two-thirds full.

3. Bake at 350° for 23 to 25 minutes or until a wooden pick inserted in center comes out clean. Cool in pans on a wire rack 5 minutes. Remove from pans to wire rack, and cool completely (about 30 minutes).

Note: Muffins may be made ahead and frozen in a zip-top plastic freezer bag up to 1 month, if desired. Remove from bag, and let thaw at room temperature.

GINGERBREAD MUFFINS WITH SPICED NUT STREUSEL

*Bake these easy, melt-in-your-mouth muffins ahead of time,
let them cool, and freeze up to one month. Reheat muffins in the
oven or microwave for a fast breakfast snack to go.*

makes 1 dozen muffins   hands-on 15 min.   total 55 min.

Spiced Nut Streusel:
¼   cup firmly packed dark brown sugar
1   Tbsp. all-purpose flour
¾   tsp. ground cinnamon
⅛   tsp. ground cloves
½   cup lightly toasted chopped pecans
1   Tbsp. butter, melted

Muffins:
2½ cups all-purpose flour
⅓   cup chopped crystallized ginger
¾   tsp. baking soda
½   tsp. table salt
½   tsp. ground cinnamon
⅛   tsp. ground cloves
¼   cup butter, softened
¼   cup granulated sugar
¼   cup firmly packed dark brown sugar
½   cup unsweetened applesauce
2   large eggs
1   cup hot brewed coffee
⅓   cup unsulfured molasses
12 paper baking cups
Vegetable cooking spray

1. Preheat oven to 350°. **Prepare Spiced Nut Streusel:** Stir together brown sugar, flour, cinnamon, and cloves in a small bowl; stir in pecans and melted butter until mixture is crumbly.

2. Prepare Muffins: Process flour and next 5 ingredients in a food processor until ginger is finely ground (about 1 minute). Beat butter at medium speed with a heavy-duty electric stand mixer until creamy. Gradually add sugars, beating until light and fluffy. Beat in applesauce until blended. Add eggs, 1 at a time, beating just until blended after each addition.

3. Combine hot brewed coffee and molasses in a 2-cup glass measuring cup. Add flour mixture to butter mixture alternately with coffee mixture, beginning and ending with flour mixture. Beat at low speed just until blended after each addition.

4. Place 12 paper baking cups in a 12-cup muffin pan, and coat cups with cooking spray. Spoon batter into cups, filling almost full. Sprinkle with Spiced Nut Streusel.

5. Bake at 350° for 18 to 20 minutes or until a wooden pick inserted in center comes out clean. Remove from pan to a wire rack, and cool 10 minutes. Serve warm.

BLUEBERRY MUFFINS WITH LEMON-CREAM CHEESE GLAZE

These aren't your ordinary blueberry muffins! The tart-and-sugary glaze turns plain blueberry muffins into extraordinary ones.

makes 1½ dozen muffins   hands-on 15 min.   total 40 min.

3½ cups all-purpose flour
1   cup sugar
1   Tbsp. baking powder
1½ tsp. table salt
3   large eggs
1½ cups milk

½   cup butter, melted
2   cups fresh or frozen blueberries
1   Tbsp. all-purpose flour
Lemon-Cream Cheese Glaze
Garnish: lemon zest

1. Preheat oven to 450º. Stir together first 4 ingredients. Whisk together eggs and next 2 ingredients; add to flour mixture, stirring just until dry ingredients are moistened. Toss blueberries with 1 Tbsp. flour, and gently fold into batter. Spoon mixture into 1½ lightly greased 12-cup muffin pans, filling three-fourths full.

2. Bake at 450º for 14 to 15 minutes or until lightly browned and a wooden pick inserted into center comes out clean. Immediately remove from pans to wire racks, and let cool 10 minutes.

3. Meanwhile, prepare Lemon-Cream Cheese Glaze. Drizzle over warm muffins.

LEMON-CREAM CHEESE GLAZE

1   (3-oz.) package cream cheese, softened
1   tsp. loosely packed lemon zest
1   Tbsp. fresh lemon juice

¼   tsp. vanilla extract
1½ cups sifted powdered sugar

Beat cream cheese at medium speed with an electric mixer until creamy. Add lemon zest and next 2 ingredients; beat until smooth. Gradually add powdered sugar, beating until smooth. **Makes about ¾ cup.**

CARAMEL APPLE MUFFINS

These are prettiest the day they are made. After standing overnight, the caramel melts into the muffins. (They're still delicious!)

makes 1 dozen muffins   hands-on 30 min.   total 1 hour, 30 min.

Cinnamon Topping:
⅓ cup firmly packed light brown sugar
1½ Tbsp. all-purpose flour
¼ tsp. ground cinnamon
1½ Tbsp. butter

Muffins:
1 (8-oz.) container sour cream
1 cup sugar
2 large eggs
1 Tbsp. vanilla extract
2 cups all-purpose flour

2 tsp. baking powder
½ tsp. baking soda
½ tsp. table salt
2 cups peeled and diced Granny Smith apples
1 (14-oz.) package caramels
3 Tbsp. whipping cream
1 cup chopped lightly salted, roasted pecans
Wax paper
Food-safe twigs or craft sticks

1. Preheat oven to 375°. **Prepare Cinnamon Topping:** Stir together brown sugar, flour, and cinnamon in a small bowl. Cut in butter with pastry blender or fork until mixture is crumbly.

2. Prepare Muffins: Beat sour cream and next 3 ingredients at low speed with an electric mixer 30 seconds or until blended.

3. Stir together flour and next 3 ingredients. Add to sour cream mixture, beating at low speed just until blended. (Do not overmix.) Stir in diced apples. Spoon into a lightly greased 12-cup muffin pan, filling three-fourths full; sprinkle with Cinnamon Topping.

4. Bake at 375° for 18 to 20 minutes or until golden brown and a wooden pick inserted in center comes out clean. Immediately remove from pan to wire rack; cool completely (about 30 minutes).

5. Microwave caramels and cream in a microwave-safe bowl at HIGH 1 to 2 minutes or until smooth, stirring at 30-second intervals. Let mixture stand, stirring occasionally, 5 minutes or until thick enough to coat muffins.

6. Quickly dip bottom three-fourths of each muffin into caramel mixture; roll bottom half of caramel-coated portion of muffin in chopped pecans, and place muffins, caramel sides up, on lightly greased wax paper. (If caramel mixture begins to harden before you've dipped all the muffins, microwave mixture a few seconds to soften.) Insert food-safe twigs or craft sticks into caramel-covered portions of muffins.

PEACH-PECAN MUFFINS

Topped with a sweet pecan crumble, these muffins are packed with peaches. Use fresh, diced Southern peaches in the peak of summer, or use thawed frozen ones in a pinch.

makes 1 dozen muffins   hands-on 20 min.   total 50 min.

Pecan Streusel:
½ cup chopped pecans
⅓ cup firmly packed brown sugar
¼ cup all-purpose flour
2 Tbsp. melted butter
1 tsp. ground cinnamon

Muffins:
1½ cups all-purpose flour
½ cup granulated sugar

2 tsp. baking powder
1 tsp. ground cinnamon
¼ tsp. table salt
½ cup butter, melted
¼ cup milk
1 large egg
1 cup fresh or frozen sliced peaches, thawed and diced
12 paper baking cups
Vegetable cooking spray

1. Prepare Pecan Streusel: Stir together pecans and next 4 ingredients until crumbly.

2. Prepare Muffins: Preheat oven to 400°. Combine flour and next 4 ingredients in a large bowl; make a well in center of mixture. Stir together butter, milk, and egg; add to dry ingredients, stirring just until moistened. Gently stir in peaches.

3. Place paper baking cups in 1 (12-cup) muffin pan, and coat with cooking spray; spoon batter into cups, filling two-thirds full. Sprinkle with Pecan Streusel.

4. Bake at 400° for 20 to 25 minutes or until a wooden pick inserted in center comes out clean. Cool in pan on a wire rack 10 minutes; remove from pan, and serve warm or at room temperature.

XXXXXXXXXXXXXXXXXXXXXXXXXXXXXXXXXXXXX

sweet idea

Nothing says you care like a basket full of freshly
baked treats. Assemble these muffins alongside
fresh peaches, peach preserves, and a small spreader.

XXXXXXXXXXXXXXXXXXXXXXXXXXXXXXXXXXXXX

green tomatoes

Whether cooked down into a relish, sliced fresh and marinated, or crispy-fried in a golden stack, green tomatoes are summer's chameleons. If you let them linger on the vine, the sun will transform them into a rainbow of juicy ripeness. However, if a frost is looming and they must be harvested when still firm and green, don't fret! They are still ripe for transformation—they just need the help of a tried-and-true recipe that celebrates their bright and fresh flavor.

SWEET GREEN TOMATO CORNMEAL MUFFINS

If you're looking for a way to use up all your green tomatoes, think beyond the deep fryer, and look to these sweet cornbread muffins with tart green tomatoes baked right inside.

makes about 2 dozen muffins   hands-on 30 min.   total 1 hour, 20 min.

2   cups seeded, diced green tomatoes (about ¾ lb.)
½   cup sugar, divided
½   cup butter, melted and divided
2   cups self-rising white cornmeal mix
2   tsp. loosely packed lemon zest
5   large eggs
1   (16-oz.) container sour cream
Vegetable cooking spray

1. Preheat oven to 450°. Sauté tomatoes and 2 Tbsp. sugar in 2 Tbsp. melted butter in a large skillet over medium-high heat 10 to 12 minutes or until tomatoes begin to caramelize and turn light brown.

2. Stir together cornmeal mix, lemon zest, and remaining 6 Tbsp. sugar in a large bowl; make a well in center of mixture. Whisk together eggs, sour cream, and remaining 6 Tbsp. butter; add to cornmeal mixture, stirring just until dry ingredients are moistened. Fold in tomatoes.

3. Generously coat small (¼ cup) brioche molds or muffin pans with cooking spray; spoon batter into molds, filling two-thirds full. Bake at 450° for 15 to 17 minutes or until a wooden pick inserted in center comes out clean. Cool in pans on a wire rack 5 minutes. Remove from pans to wire rack, and cool completely (about 30 minutes).

xxxxxxxxxxxxxxxxxxxxxxxxxxxxxxxxxxx

sweet idea

Serve with fresh basil butter: Stir together ½ cup softened butter and 2 Tbsp. finely chopped fresh basil.

xxxxxxxxxxxxxxxxxxxxxxxxxxxxxxxxxxx

FRESH ROSEMARY MUFFINS

Redolent with fragrant rosemary, these savory, crowd-pleasing muffins boast a tangy goat cheese filling and are as delicious with a holiday roast as with eggs and a side of bacon.

makes 1 dozen muffins   hands-on 15 min.   total 38 min.

¾ cup milk
¼ cup golden raisins
¼ cup raisins
¼ cup currants
1   Tbsp. chopped fresh rosemary
¼ cup unsalted butter

1½ cups all-purpose flour
½ cup sugar
2   tsp. baking powder
¼ tsp. table salt
1   large egg, lightly beaten
4   oz. goat cheese

1. Preheat oven to 350°. Cook first 5 ingredients in a heavy saucepan over medium heat, stirring often, 2 minutes or just until mixture begins to steam; remove from heat. Add butter; stir until butter melts. Cool completely.

2. Combine flour and next 3 ingredients in a large bowl; make a well in center of mixture. Stir together egg and milk mixture until well blended; add to flour mixture, stirring just until moistened.

3. Spoon one-third of batter into 1 lightly greased 12-cup muffin pan; add 2 tsp. goat cheese to each muffin cup. Spoon remaining batter over goat cheese, filling each cup two-thirds full.

4. Bake at 350° for 20 to 24 minutes or until golden brown. Cool in pan on a wire rack 3 minutes. Remove from pan.

Praline-Apple
Bread

Apricot-Pecan
Bread

Mini Banana-
Cranberry-Nut
Bread Loaves

Lemon-Poppy Seed
Zucchini Bread

PRALINE~APPLE BREAD

(*pictured on page 124*)

Whether you say "pray-leen" or "prah-leen," you will love this sweet loaf. Sour cream is the secret to its rich, moist texture. There's no butter or oil in the batter—only in the glaze.

makes 1 loaf   hands-on 20 min.   total 2 hours, 30 min.

1 (8-oz.) container sour cream	½ tsp. table salt
1 cup granulated sugar	1½ cups finely chopped, peeled
2 large eggs	Granny Smith apples (about ¾ lb.)
1 Tbsp. vanilla extract	1½ cups chopped toasted pecans, divided
2 cups all-purpose flour	½ cup butter
2 tsp. baking powder	½ cup firmly packed light brown sugar
½ tsp. baking soda	

1. Preheat oven to 350°. Beat first 4 ingredients at low speed with an electric mixer 2 minutes or until blended.

2. Stir together flour and next 3 ingredients. Add to sour cream mixture, beating just until blended. Stir in apples and ½ cup toasted pecans. Spoon batter into a greased and floured 9- x 5-inch loaf pan. Sprinkle with remaining 1 cup chopped pecans; lightly press pecans into batter.

3. Bake at 350° for 1 hour to 1 hour and 5 minutes or until a wooden pick inserted into center comes out clean, shielding with aluminum foil after 50 minutes to prevent excessive browning. Cool in pan on a wire rack 10 minutes; remove from pan to wire rack.

4. Bring butter and brown sugar to a boil in a 1-qt. heavy saucepan over medium heat, stirring constantly; boil 1 minute. Remove from heat, and spoon over top of bread; let cool completely.

APRICOT~PECAN BREAD

(pictured on page 124)

This quick bread has a cake-like consistency thanks to the step of creaming the butter and sugar. Over two cups of apricots adds lots of flavor and texture while ensuring the bread stays moist, even if made a day or two ahead.

makes 2 loaves   hands-on 15 min.   total 3 hours, 15 min.

2½ cups dried apricots, chopped	2 large eggs
1 cup chopped toasted pecans	1 Tbsp. plus 1 tsp. baking powder
4 cups all-purpose flour, divided	½ tsp. baking soda
¼ cup butter, softened	½ tsp. table salt
2 cups sugar	1½ cups orange juice

1. Combine chopped apricots and warm water to cover in a large bowl; let stand 30 minutes. Drain apricots. Stir in pecans and ½ cup flour; set aside.

2. Beat butter at medium speed with an electric mixer 2 minutes; gradually add sugar, beating until light and fluffy. Add eggs, 1 at a time, beating after each addition.

3. Combine remaining 3½ cups flour, baking powder, baking soda, and salt. Add to butter mixture alternately with orange juice, beginning and ending with flour mixture. Stir in apricot mixture.

4. Preheat oven to 350°. Spoon batter into 2 greased and floured 8- x 4-inch loaf pans; let stand at room temperature 20 minutes.

5. Bake at 350° for 1 hour or until a wooden pick inserted in center comes out clean. Cool in pans on a wire rack 10 to 15 minutes; remove from pans, and cool completely on wire rack.

~§§§ BAKING SECRETS §§§~
from the Southern Living Test Kitchen

To get perfect slices of quick breads, let the bread cool completely and then cut with a serrated or electric knife.

MINI BANANA~ CRANBERRY~NUT BREAD LOAVES

(pictured on page 125)

These loaves may become your new holiday breakfast, or even gifting, tradition! Loaded up with cranberries and pecans with a citrus glaze, this is not your ordinary banana bread.

makes 5 miniature loaves   hands-on 25 min.   total 1 hour, 25 min.

1	(8-oz.) package cream cheese, softened	½	tsp. table salt
¾	cup butter, softened	1½	cups mashed ripe bananas
2	cups sugar	¾	cup chopped fresh cranberries
2	large eggs	½	tsp. vanilla extract
3	cups all-purpose flour	¾	cup chopped toasted pecans
½	tsp. baking powder		Orange Glaze
½	tsp. baking soda		

1. Preheat oven to 350°. Beat cream cheese and butter at medium speed with an electric mixer until creamy. Gradually add sugar, beating until light and fluffy. Add eggs, 1 at a time, beating just until blended after each addition.

2. Combine flour and next 3 ingredients; gradually add to butter mixture, beating at low speed just until blended. Stir in bananas, next 2 ingredients, and pecans. Spoon about 1½ cups batter into each of 5 greased and floured 5- x 3-inch miniature loaf pans.

3. Bake at 350° for 40 to 44 minutes or until a wooden pick inserted in center comes out clean and sides pull away from pans. Cool in pans 10 minutes. Transfer to wire racks. Prepare Orange Glaze. Drizzle over warm bread loaves, and cool 10 minutes.

Regular-Size Banana-Cranberry-Nut Bread Loaves:

Spoon batter into 2 greased and floured 8- x 4-inch loaf pans. Bake at 350° for 1 hour and 10 minutes or until a wooden pick inserted in center comes out clean. **Makes 2 loaves.**

ORANGE GLAZE

A drizzle of this glaze adds a citrusy, sweet topping to your favorite bread, sweet roll, or coffee cake.

1	cup powdered sugar	2	to 3 Tbsp. fresh orange juice
1	tsp. loosely packed orange zest		

Stir together powdered sugar and remaining ingredients in a small bowl until blended. Use immediately. **Makes ½ cup.**

LEMON~POPPY SEED ZUCCHINI BREAD

(pictured on page 125)

The tender, fine-crumbed texture and bright lemon flavor
offer a refreshing change from traditional spiced zucchini breads.

makes 3 miniature loaves   hands-on 25 min.   total 2 hours, 15 min.

½	cup butter, softened	⅛	tsp. baking soda
1⅓	cups sugar	½	cup sour cream
3	large eggs	1	cup shredded zucchini
1½	cups all-purpose flour	1	Tbsp. loosely packed lemon zest
½	tsp. table salt	2	tsp. poppy seeds

1. Preheat oven to 325°. Beat butter at medium speed with a heavy-duty electric stand mixer until creamy. Gradually add sugar, beating until light and fluffy. Add eggs, 1 at a time, beating just until blended after each addition.

2. Stir together flour, salt, and baking soda. Add to butter mixture alternately with sour cream, beginning and ending with flour mixture. Beat at low speed just until blended after each addition. Stir in zucchini and next 2 ingredients. Spoon batter into 3 greased and floured 5- x 3-inch disposable aluminum foil miniature loaf pans (about 1⅓ cups batter per pan).

3. Bake at 325° for 40 to 45 minutes or until a wooden pick inserted in center comes out clean. Cool in pans on wire racks 10 minutes; remove from pans to wire racks, and allow to cool completely.

xxxxxxxxxxxxxxxxxxxxxxxxxxxxxxxxxxxxx

sweet idea

These lovely little loaves are the sweetest way to
greet a new neighbor or thank a host for
a dinner party. Just wrap cooled loaves in plastic wrap
before tying up with wide ribbon and a tag.

xxxxxxxxxxxxxxxxxxxxxxxxxxxxxxxxxxxxx

~ brown sugar ~

One of the South's favorite sweeteners is cane sugar,
pressed from the sugar cane that grows in the
Deep South. As the sugar is processed, it can take
many forms, from granulated sugars to rich syrups.
Brown sugar combines two of these—granulated white
sugar and molasses. More flavorful and softer
than white sugar, light brown sugar has a little molasses
added while dark brown sugar has more.

CLASSIC BANANA BREAD

*No collection of Southern quick breads would be complete without
the most traditional and dependable banana bread. A little lemon juice
balances the sweet bananas, while we've used a combination of
white and light brown sugar to complement, not overpower, the bananas.*

makes 1 loaf   hands-on 30 min.   total 2 hours, 25 min.

1¾ cups all-purpose flour	½ cup unsalted butter, softened
1 tsp. baking soda	½ cup granulated sugar
½ tsp. table salt	½ cup firmly packed light brown sugar
½ tsp. ground cinnamon	½ tsp. vanilla extract
3 very ripe bananas (about 1 lb.)	2 large eggs
1 tsp. fresh lemon juice	¼ cup buttermilk

1. Preheat oven to 350°. Sift together first 4 ingredients in a large bowl. Mash bananas with lemon juice in a small bowl. (You want a little texture—like semi lumpy mashed potatoes.)

2. Beat butter and next 3 ingredients at low speed with a heavy-duty electric stand mixer 1 minute or until combined. Increase speed to medium, and beat 1½ to 2 minutes or until light and fluffy. Add eggs, 1 at a time, beating until blended after each addition, stopping to scrape bowl as needed.

3. Add flour mixture to butter mixture alternately with buttermilk, beginning and ending with flour mixture. Beat at low speed just until blended after each addition. Add banana mixture, beating just until batter is blended (no more than 10 seconds). Pour batter into a well-buttered and floured 8- x 4-inch loaf pan, and place on a baking sheet.

4. Bake at 350° for 55 to 60 minutes or until a long wooden pick inserted in center comes out clean. Cool in pan on a wire rack 10 minutes. Remove from pan to a wire rack, and cool 50 minutes. Wrap in plastic wrap (it will still be warm—this helps the bread stay moist), and store at room temperature up to 4 days.

⁓⁂ BAKING SECRETS ⁂⁓
from the Southern Living Test Kitchen

*If you have more overripe bananas than you can use,
freeze them to use later in banana bread, waffles,
or smoothies. Peel bananas, place them in a zip-top plastic
freezer bag, and freeze. If using for baked goods,
be sure to thaw bananas before blending into batters.*

LEMON TEA BREAD

Tart lemons give intense flavor to this quick bread with a dense, cake-like texture. A sweet glaze ensures every slice is something worth savoring.

makes 1 (8-inch) loaf   hands-on 20 min.   total 2 hours, 30 min.

½ cup butter, softened	½ cup milk
1 cup granulated sugar	2 Tbsp. loosely packed lemon zest, divided
2 large eggs	
1½ cups all-purpose flour	1 cup powdered sugar
1 tsp. baking powder	2 Tbsp. fresh lemon juice
½ tsp. table salt	1 Tbsp. granulated sugar

1. Preheat oven to 350°. Beat softened butter at medium speed with an electric mixer until creamy. Gradually add 1 cup granulated sugar, beating until light and fluffy. Add eggs, 1 at a time, beating just until blended after each addition.

2. Stir together flour, baking powder, and salt; add to butter mixture alternately with milk, beating at low speed just until blended, beginning and ending with flour mixture. Stir in 1 Tbsp. lemon zest. Spoon batter into a greased and floured 8- x 4-inch loaf pan.

3. Bake at 350° for 1 hour or until a wooden pick inserted in center of bread comes out clean. Let cool in pan 10 minutes. Remove bread from pan, and cool completely on a wire rack.

4. Stir together powdered sugar and lemon juice until smooth; spoon evenly over top of bread, letting excess drip down sides. Stir together remaining 1 Tbsp. lemon zest and 1 Tbsp. granulated sugar; sprinkle on top of bread.

Lemon-Almond Tea Bread: Stir ½ tsp. almond extract into batter. Proceed as directed.

SPICED PEACH~ CARROT BREAD

This moist, flavorful bread recipe won first place in the side-dish category in South Carolina's 2009 Annual Peach-Off contest.

makes 1 loaf   hands-on 15 min.   total 2 hours, 25 min.

2½ cups all-purpose flour
1   cup sugar
1   tsp. ground cinnamon
¾   tsp. baking soda
½   tsp. baking powder
½   tsp. table salt
¼   tsp. ground nutmeg

1½ cups peeled and chopped fresh, ripe peaches
¾   cup freshly grated carrots
⅔   cup vegetable oil
½   cup milk
2   large eggs, lightly beaten
¾   cup toasted chopped pecans

1. Preheat oven to 350°. Stir together flour and next 6 ingredients in a large bowl; add peaches, next 4 ingredients, and toasted pecans, stirring just until dry ingredients are moistened. Spoon batter into a lightly greased 9- x 5-inch loaf pan.

2. Bake at 350° for 1 hour and 5 minutes to 1 hour and 10 minutes or until a long wooden pick inserted in center comes out clean. Cool in pan on a wire rack 5 minutes. Remove from pan to wire rack, and cool completely (about 1 hour).

BAKING SECRETS
from the Southern Living Test Kitchen

When grating carrots, it's easiest to work with firm, crisp carrots. Store them in the refrigerator to keep them fresh. If carrots seem a little limp, revive them by soaking in ice water for 20 to 30 minutes.

CREAM CHEESE-BANANA-NUT BREAD

Enjoy banana bread without all the guilt with this healthy recipe. Expect a denser bread:
It won't rise as much as traditional breads, and the texture will be very moist.

makes 2 loaves   hands-on 15 min.   total 2 hours

¼   cup butter, softened
1   (8-oz.) package ⅓-less-fat cream cheese,
      softened
1   cup sugar
2   large eggs
1½ cups whole wheat flour
1½ cups all-purpose flour
½   tsp. baking powder

½   tsp. baking soda
½   tsp. table salt
1   cup buttermilk
1½ cups mashed very ripe bananas
      (1¼ lb. unpeeled bananas, about
      4 medium)
1¼ cups toasted chopped pecans, divided
½   tsp. vanilla extract

1. Preheat oven to 350°. Beat butter and cream cheese at medium speed with an electric mixer until creamy. Gradually add sugar, beating until light and fluffy. Add eggs, 1 at a time, beating just until blended after each addition.

2. Combine whole wheat flour and next 4 ingredients; gradually add to butter mixture alternately with buttermilk, beginning and ending with flour mixture. Beat at low speed just until blended after each addition. Stir in bananas, ¾ cup toasted pecans, and vanilla. Spoon batter into 2 greased and floured 8- x 4-inch loaf pans. Sprinkle with remaining ½ cup pecans.

3. Bake at 350° for 1 hour or until a long wooden pick inserted in center comes out clean and sides of bread pull away from pan, shielding with aluminum foil during last 15 minutes to prevent excessive browning, if necessary. Cool bread in pans on wire racks 10 minutes. Remove from pans to wire racks. Let cool 30 minutes.

Note: If you've never worked with whole wheat flour, accurate measuring is everything. Be sure to spoon the flour into a dry measuring cup (do not pack) rather than scooping the cup into the flour, and level it off with a straight edge.

Cinnamon-Cream Cheese-Banana-Nut Bread: Prepare recipe as directed through Step 2, omitting pecans sprinkled over batter. Stir together ¼ cup firmly packed brown sugar, ¼ cup chopped pecans (not toasted), 1½ tsp. all-purpose flour, 1½ tsp. melted butter, and ¼ to ½ tsp. ground cinnamon. Lightly sprinkle mixture over batter in pans. Bake and cool as directed.

Peanut Butter-Cream Cheese-Banana-Nut Bread: Prepare recipe as directed through Step 2, omitting pecans sprinkled over batter. Combine ¼ cup all-purpose flour and ¼ cup firmly packed brown sugar in a small bowl. Cut in 2 Tbsp. creamy peanut butter and 1½ tsp. butter with pastry blender or fork until mixture resembles small peas. Lightly sprinkle mixture over batter in pans. Bake and cool as directed.

CHEDDAR~CHIVE BEER BREAD

With minimal prep, you can enjoy this homemade beer bread loaf.
Take about 5 minutes to mix the ingredients, pop in the oven, and then enjoy!
Incorporate your favorite local Southern brew for a down-home twist.

makes 1 loaf   hands-on 5 min.   total 1 hour

3 cups self-rising flour	1 (12-oz.) bottle pale ale
½ cup sugar	(such as SweetWater 420 Extra Pale Ale)*
¾ cup shredded sharp Cheddar cheese	¼ cup butter, melted
2 Tbsp. chopped fresh chives	

1. Preheat oven to 350°. Stir together first 4 ingredients; stir in beer. Pour into a lightly greased 9- x 5-inch loaf pan.

2. Bake at 350° for 45 minutes. Pour melted butter over top. Bake 10 more minutes.

* Nonalcoholic or light beer may be substituted.

xxxxxxxxxxxxxxxxxxxxxxxxxxxxxxxxxx

sweet idea

Make this easy, flavorful bread recipe to pair with
an appetizing dip or a hearty bowl of soup.

xxxxxxxxxxxxxxxxxxxxxxxxxxxxxxxxxx

GLUTEN~FREE
BANANA~NUT BREAD

Even if you're following a gluten-free diet or baking for someone who is, you can still enjoy banana-nut bread. The combination of brown rice flour and sorghum flour imparts a tender crumb and texture that you'll find in a traditional banana bread.

makes 1 loaf   hands-on 15 min.   total 2 hours, 35 min.

1	cup boiling water	1½	cups brown rice flour
½	cup chopped dates	½	cup sorghum flour
4	large eggs	1	tsp. baking soda
2	cups mashed, very ripe bananas (about 4)	½	tsp. table salt
¾	cup granulated sugar	¼	tsp. ground nutmeg
½	cup unsweetened applesauce	⅓	cup butter, melted
1	tsp. vanilla extract	½	cup chopped walnuts

1. Preheat oven to 350°. Pour 1 cup boiling water over dates in a small bowl. Let stand 10 minutes. Drain and pat dry.

2. Lightly beat eggs with a whisk in a large bowl. Whisk in bananas and next 3 ingredients until blended.

3. Stir together brown rice flour and next 4 ingredients in a small bowl. Gently stir flour mixture into egg mixture, stirring just until blended. Gently stir in melted butter, walnuts, and dates. Spoon mixture into a lightly greased 9- x 5-inch loaf pan.

4. Bake at 350° for 1 hour to 1 hour and 10 minutes or until a wooden pick inserted in center comes out clean. Cool in pan on a wire rack 10 minutes. Remove from pan to wire rack, and cool completely (about 1 hour).

BAKING SECRETS
from the Southern Living Test Kitchen

For best results, use a light-colored pan. Or, turn your dark pan into a shiny one by wrapping the outside of it with heavy-duty aluminum foil, shiny side out.

cakes
& coffee cakes

CAKES

*Become a better cake baker with the help of these insider tips
and techniques for perfect cakes every time.*

While every step of making a cake can be important, the following techniques are the most common sticking points for most beginner bakers. Avoid complete re-dos by separating eggs successfully, creaming butter and sugar to give cakes a light-as-air texture, and folding meringue into batter without deflating it. Once you've got the batter made, bake cake layers evenly and level tops before frosting them with ease.

⋯⋯⋯ *separating eggs* ⋯⋯⋯

Step 1: Use fresh cold or room temperature eggs, depending on recipe.

Step 2: Crack egg. Transfer yolk back and forth between shells, allowing white to drip into bowl. Check egg white for traces of yolk.

Step 3: Gently place separated egg yolk in a second bowl, and proceed with recipe.

⋯⋯⋯ *creaming butter & sugar* ⋯⋯⋯

Step 1: For maximum volume, start with all ingredients at room temperature.

Step 2: Beat softened butter and sugar for 5 to 7 minutes at medium speed with an electric mixer.

Step 3: Mixture should be very light and fluffy.

......folding in meringue......

Step 1: Place one-third of beaten egg whites into batter.

Step 2: Fold egg whites up and through center of batter.

Step 3: Fold batter until there are no visible signs of egg whites.

......baking & leveling......

Step 1: Test for doneness by inserting a toothpick into the center. It should come out clean.

Step 2: Using a long serrated knife, cut off top in a sawing motion, keeping the knife parallel to the surface.

Step 3: Discard cake top or save for another use.

......frosting......

Step 1: Stack up cake layers and frosting on a rotating pedestal. Place pieces of wax paper under sides for easy cleanup.

Step 2: Dollop frosting on top of cake, and smooth out a thin layer over sides and top.

Step 3: Once cake is covered in a thin layer of frosting, refrigerate for 30 minutes so frosting sets and cake is stable.

Step 4: Dollop more frosting onto cake, and smooth out over sides and top.

PUMPKIN CUPCAKES WITH BROWNED BUTTER FROSTING

While many pumpkin cakes feature a cream cheese frosting or glaze, we've updated this fall favorite with a rich frosting flavored with browned butter and vanilla paste. For a generous swirl of frosting on each cupcake, double the recipe for Browned Butter Frosting.

makes 30 cupcakes   hands-on 30 min.   total 2 hours, 30 min., including frosting

30	paper baking cups	1	cup buttermilk
1	cup butter, softened	1	tsp. baking soda
2	cups sugar	1	cup chopped toasted pecans
5	large eggs, separated	1	cup canned pumpkin
1½	tsp. pumpkin pie spice		Browned Butter Frosting
3	cups all-purpose flour, divided		

1. Preheat oven to 350°. Place 30 paper baking cups in 3 (12-cup) standard-size muffin pans.

2. Beat butter at medium speed with a heavy-duty electric stand mixer until creamy. Gradually add sugar, beating until light and fluffy. Add egg yolks, 1 at a time, beating just until blended after each addition.

3. Stir together pumpkin pie spice and 2¾ cups flour in a medium bowl; stir together buttermilk and baking soda in a small bowl. Add flour mixture to butter mixture alternately with buttermilk mixture, beginning and ending with flour mixture. Beat at low speed just until blended after each addition.

4. Stir together pecans and remaining ¼ cup flour. Fold pecan mixture and pumpkin into batter.

5. Beat egg whites at high speed with an electric mixer until stiff peaks form. Stir about one-third of egg whites into batter; fold in remaining egg whites. Spoon batter into muffin cups, filling about three-fourths full.

6. Bake at 350° for 18 to 22 minutes or until a wooden pick inserted in center comes out clean. Remove from pans to wire rack, and cool completely, about 20 minutes before frosting.

BROWNED BUTTER FROSTING

1½	cups butter	6	Tbsp. milk
7½	cups powdered sugar	1½	tsp. vanilla bean paste

1. Cook 1½ cups butter in a medium-size saucepan over medium heat, stirring constantly, 8 to 10 minutes or just until butter begins to turn golden brown; pour butter into a small bowl. Cover and chill 1 hour or until butter is cool and begins to solidify.

2. Beat browned butter at medium speed with an electric mixer until fluffy; gradually add powdered sugar alternately with milk, beginning and ending with sugar. Beat at low speed until well blended after each addition. Add in vanilla bean paste, and beat at medium speed for 5 minutes or until fluffy. **Makes about 3 cups.**

RED VELVET CUPCAKES

These moist, dense cupcakes are as luxurious as they sound—complete with their signature red color and to-die-for White Chocolate-Amaretto Frosting.

makes 2 dozen cupcakes   hands-on 25 min.   total 2 hours, 18 min.

¾ cup butter, softened
1½ cups sugar
3 large eggs
1 (1-oz.) bottle red liquid food coloring
1 tsp. vanilla extract
2½ cups all-purpose flour
3 Tbsp. unsweetened cocoa

½ tsp. table salt
1 cup buttermilk
1 Tbsp. white vinegar
1 tsp. baking soda
Paper baking cups
White Chocolate-Amaretto Frosting
Garnish: white chocolate shavings

1. Preheat oven to 350°. Beat butter at medium speed with an electric mixer until fluffy; gradually add sugar, beating well. Add eggs, 1 at a time, beating until blended after each addition. Stir in food coloring and vanilla until blended.

2. Combine flour, cocoa, and salt. Stir together buttermilk, vinegar, and baking soda in a 4-cup liquid measuring cup. (Mixture will bubble.) Add flour mixture to butter mixture alternately with buttermilk mixture, beginning and ending with flour mixture. Beat at low speed until blended after each addition. Place 24 paper baking cups in 2 (12-cup) muffin pans; spoon batter into cups, filling three-fourths full.

3. Bake at 350° for 18 to 20 minutes or until a wooden pick inserted in centers comes out clean. Remove cupcakes from pans to wire racks, and let cool completely (about 45 minutes).

4. Pipe or spread frosting onto cupcakes.

WHITE CHOCOLATE-AMARETTO FROSTING

2 (4-oz.) white chocolate baking bars
⅓ cup heavy cream
1 cup butter, softened

6 cups powdered sugar, divided
¼ cup almond liqueur

1. Break white chocolate baking bars into pieces. Melt white chocolate and cream in a microwave-safe bowl at MEDIUM (50% power) 1 minute or until melted and smooth, stirring at 30-second intervals. (Do not overheat.) Let cool to room temperature (about 30 minutes).

2. Beat butter and 1 cup powdered sugar at low speed with an electric mixer until blended. Add 5 cups powdered sugar alternately with almond liqueur, beating at low speed until blended after each addition. Add white chocolate mixture; beat at medium speed until spreading consistency. **Makes 4 cups.**

COCONUT-PECAN CUPCAKES

Small bites are big treats! Mini versions of this Southern classic equal guilt-free enjoyment. The Caramel Frosting crown on these cupcakes takes the cherished combination of coconut and pecans over the top in this after-dinner treat.

makes 3 dozen cupcakes   hands-on 20 min.   total 2 hours, 15 min.

½ cup butter, softened
½ cup shortening
2 cups sugar
5 large eggs, separated
1 Tbsp. vanilla extract
2 cups all-purpose flour
1 tsp. baking soda

1 cup buttermilk
1 cup sweetened flaked coconut
1 cup toasted finely chopped pecans
Paper baking cups
Caramel Frosting
Garnish: chopped roasted salted pecans, sweetened flaked coconut

1. Preheat oven to 350°. Beat butter and shortening at medium speed with an electric mixer until fluffy; gradually add sugar, beating well. Add egg yolks, 1 at a time, beating until blended after each addition. Add vanilla; beat until blended.

2. Combine flour and baking soda; add to butter mixture alternately with buttermilk, beginning and ending with flour mixture. Beat at low speed just until blended after each addition. Stir in coconut and pecans.

3. Beat egg whites at high speed until stiff peaks form, and fold into batter. Place 36 paper baking cups in 3 (12-cup) muffin pans; spoon batter into cups, filling half full.

4. Bake at 350° for 18 to 20 minutes or until a wooden pick inserted in centers comes out clean. Remove from pans to wire racks, and let cool completely (about 45 minutes).

5. Pipe frosting onto cupcakes.

CARAMEL FROSTING

1 (14-oz.) package caramels
½ cup heavy cream
1 cup butter, softened

5 cups powdered sugar
2 tsp. vanilla extract

1. Microwave caramels and cream in a microwave-safe bowl at HIGH 1 minute; stir. Continue to microwave at 30-second intervals, stirring until caramels melt and mixture is smooth. Let cool until lukewarm (about 30 minutes).

2. Beat butter at medium speed with an electric mixer until creamy. Gradually add powdered sugar alternately with caramel mixture, beating at low speed until blended and smooth after each addition. Stir in vanilla. **Makes 4½ cups.**

LEMON CURD~FILLED ANGEL FOOD CUPCAKES

A recipe for Angel Food Cake, a classic sponge cake, first appeared in The Kentucky Housewife cookbook in 1839, and delicious twists on the recipe continue. Here, miniature cakes are filled with a tangy lemon curd and topped with Cream Cheese Frosting. Garnish with lemon zest for an impressive presentation.

makes 1 dozen cupcakes   hands-on 30 min.   total 1 hour, 47 min.

1¾ cups plus 2 Tbsp. sugar
1⅓ cups all-purpose flour
¼ tsp. table salt
2 tsp. lemon juice
½ tsp. vanilla extract
½ tsp. light rum
¼ tsp. orange extract

1¾ cups large egg whites
    (about 13 to 15 large eggs)
¾ tsp. cream of tartar
1 (10-oz.) jar lemon curd
⅓ cup sour cream
Cream Cheese Frosting
Garnish: lemon zest

1. Preheat oven to 375°. Sift together sugar, flour, and salt in a bowl. Combine lemon juice, vanilla, rum, and orange extract.

2. Beat egg whites and cream of tartar at high speed with a heavy-duty electric stand mixer until stiff peaks form; gently transfer egg white mixture to a large bowl.

3. Gradually fold in sugar mixture with a large spatula, ⅓ cup at a time, folding just until blended after each addition. Fold in lemon juice mixture.

4. Arrange 12 (2½- x 2-inch) muffin-size paper baking molds* on an aluminum foil-lined baking sheet; spoon batter into baking molds, filling almost completely full.

5. Bake at 375° for 17 to 19 minutes or until a long wooden pick inserted in centers comes out clean. Transfer to a wire rack, and cool completely (about 1 hour).

6. Make a small hole in top of each cupcake using the handle of a wooden spoon. In a medium bowl, stir together lemon curd and sour cream. Spoon filling into a zip-top plastic freezer bag. Snip 1 corner of bag to make a tiny hole. Pipe a generous amount of filling into each cupcake.

7. Spread Cream Cheese Frosting on tops of cupcakes.

* 15 jumbo aluminum foil baking cups may be substituted. Place baking cups directly on an aluminum foil-lined baking sheet; fill cups, and proceed as directed.

CREAM CHEESE FROSTING

1 (8-oz.) package cream cheese, softened
3 Tbsp. butter, softened

1 Tbsp. fresh lemon juice
1½ tsp. vanilla extract
5 cups powdered sugar

Beat cream cheese and butter at medium speed with an electric mixer until creamy; add lemon juice and vanilla, beating just until blended. Gradually add powdered sugar, beating at low speed until blended. **Makes about 3 cups.**

MINI BOURBON-AND-COLA BUNDT CAKES

Use a classic Southern cocktail combo to flavor a chocolate cake by adding bourbon and cola to the cake batter and topping the mini Bundt cakes with a sweet bourbon-and-cola glaze.

makes 3 dozen mini Bundt cakes   hands-on 20 min.   total 1 hour, 22 min.

1½ cups butter, softened
2½ cups sugar
3   large eggs
1½ tsp. vanilla extract
1   cup cola soft drink
¾   cup buttermilk

½   cup bourbon
3   cups all-purpose flour
½   cup unsweetened cocoa
1½ tsp. baking soda
½   tsp. table salt
    Bourbon-and-Cola Glaze

1. Preheat oven to 350°. Beat butter at medium speed with an electric mixer until creamy. Gradually add sugar; beat until blended. Add eggs and vanilla; beat at low speed until blended.

2. Stir together cola, buttermilk, and bourbon in a small bowl. Combine flour and next 3 ingredients in another bowl. Add flour mixture to butter mixture alternately with cola mixture, beginning and ending with flour mixture. Beat at low speed just until blended after each addition, stopping to scrape bowl as needed. Pour batter into 3 lightly greased 12-cup Bundt brownie pans, filling each three-fourths full.

3. Bake at 350° for 12 to 15 minutes or until a wooden pick inserted in center comes out clean. Cool in pans on a wire rack 10 minutes. Remove from pans to wire racks, and cool 30 minutes. Drizzle warm Bourbon-and-Cola Glaze over cakes.

Bourbon-and-Cola Bundt Cake: Pour batter into 1 greased and floured 14-cup Bundt pan. Bake at 350° for 45 to 50 minutes or until a wooden pick inserted in center comes out clean.

BOURBON-AND-COLA GLAZE

¼   cup butter
3   Tbsp. cola soft drink
2½ Tbsp. unsweetened cocoa

1   Tbsp. bourbon
2   cups plus 2 Tbsp. powdered sugar

Cook first 3 ingredients in a 2-qt. saucepan over medium-low heat, stirring constantly, until butter melts. Remove from heat; stir in bourbon. Beat in powdered sugar at medium speed with an electric mixer until smooth. **Makes about 1 cup.**

BUTTERMILK POUND CAKE WITH BUTTERMILK CUSTARD SAUCE

Forget the dollop of whipped cream or scoop of ice cream; for this simple pound cake, we've doubled the dose of buttermilk with a creamy custard that soaks into the slices of cake, making it all the more heavenly.

makes 12 servings   hands on 30 min.   total 2 hours, 45 min.

1⅓ cups butter, softened
2½ cups sugar
6   large eggs
3   cups all-purpose flour

½   cup buttermilk
1   tsp. vanilla extract
Buttermilk Custard Sauce

1. Preheat oven to 325°. Beat butter at medium speed with a heavy-duty electric stand mixer until creamy. Gradually add sugar, beating at medium speed until light and fluffy. Add eggs, 1 at a time, beating just until blended after each addition.

2. Add flour to butter mixture alternately with buttermilk, beginning and ending with flour mixture. Beat at low speed just until blended after each addition. Stir in vanilla. Pour batter into a greased and floured 10-inch (14-cup) tube pan.

3. Bake at 325° for 1 hour and 5 minutes to 1 hour and 10 minutes or until a long wooden pick inserted in center comes out clean. Cool in pan on a wire rack 10 to 15 minutes; remove from pan to wire rack, and cool completely (about 1 hour). Serve with Buttermilk Custard Sauce.

BUTTERMILK CUSTARD SAUCE

2   cups buttermilk
½   cup sugar
1   Tbsp. cornstarch

3   large egg yolks
1   tsp. vanilla extract

Whisk together buttermilk, sugar, cornstarch, and egg yolks in a heavy 3-qt. saucepan. Bring to a boil over medium heat, whisking constantly, and boil 1 minute. Remove from heat, and stir in vanilla. Serve warm or cold. Store leftovers in an airtight container in refrigerator up to 1 week. **Makes about 2⅓ cups.**

Sweet Potato
Pound Cake

Ginger Pound Cake
with Glazed Cranberry
Ambrosia

Blackberry Jam
Cake

Lemon-Lime
Pound Cake

SWEET POTATO POUND CAKE

(pictured on page 158)

Bored with sweet potato casserole? Try this moist dessert, a twist on traditional pound cake that features nutrient-rich sweet potatoes. It's the perfect addition to any holiday table.

makes 10 to 12 servings   hands-on 25 min.   total 2 hours, 40 min.

1	(8-oz.) package cream cheese, softened	2	tsp. baking powder
½	cup butter, softened	1	tsp. baking soda
2	cups sugar	¼	tsp. table salt
4	large eggs	1	tsp. ground cinnamon or nutmeg
2½	cups mashed cooked sweet potatoes		(optional)
3	cups all-purpose flour	1	tsp. vanilla extract

1. Preheat oven to 350°. Beat cream cheese and butter at medium speed with a heavy-duty electric stand mixer until creamy. Gradually add sugar, beating until light and fluffy. Add eggs, 1 at a time, beating just until yellow disappears. Add sweet potatoes, and beat well.

2. Stir together flour, next 3 ingredients, and, if desired, cinnamon in a medium bowl. Gradually add flour mixture to butter mixture, beating at low speed just until blended after each addition. Stir in vanilla. Spoon batter into a greased and floured 10-inch (14-cup) tube pan.

3. Bake at 350° for 1 hour and 5 minutes to 1 hour and 10 minutes or until a long wooden pick inserted in center comes out clean. Cool in pan on a wire rack 10 minutes. Remove from pan to wire rack, and cool completely (about 1 hour).

Sweet Potato Pound Cake Loaves: Prepare batter as directed; pour into 2 greased and floured 8½- x 4½-inch loaf pans. Bake and cool as directed.

xxxxxxxxxxxxxxxxxxxxxxxxxxxxxxxxxxxxx

sweet idea

For a dessert that's over-the-top, serve slices
of this cake with scoops of cinnamon ice cream and
crumbled gingersnap cookies sprinkled on top.

xxxxxxxxxxxxxxxxxxxxxxxxxxxxxxxxxxxxx

GINGER POUND CAKE WITH GLAZED CRANBERRY AMBROSIA

(pictured on page 158)

Spicy and sweet thanks to grated fresh ginger, this pound cake is complemented by a cranberry-orange topping that also makes for a gorgeous presentation. Make the ambrosia a day ahead so it has time to set up in the refrigerator.

makes 1 (9-inch) loaf   hands-on 15 min.   total 10 hours, 40 min., including ambrosia

⅔ cup butter, softened
1 cup sugar
3 large eggs
2¼ cups all-purpose flour
1 tsp. baking powder

1 tsp. table salt
½ cup milk
2 Tbsp. minced fresh ginger
½ tsp. vanilla extract
Glazed Cranberry Ambrosia

1. Preheat oven to 325°. Beat butter at medium speed with an electric mixer 2 minutes or until creamy; gradually add sugar, and beat 5 to 7 minutes. Add eggs, 1 at a time, beating just until yellow disappears.

2. Combine flour, baking powder, and salt; add to butter mixture alternately with milk, beginning and ending with flour mixture. Beat at low speed just until blended after each addition. Stir in ginger and vanilla. Pour batter into a greased and floured 9- x 5-inch loaf pan.

3. Bake at 325° for 1 hour and 20 minutes or until a long wooden pick inserted in center comes out clean. Cool in pan on a wire rack 10 minutes; remove from pan, and cool completely on wire rack. Serve with Glazed Cranberry Ambrosia.

GLAZED CRANBERRY AMBROSIA

1 cup fresh or frozen cranberries, thawed
¼ cup sugar
1 Tbsp. minced fresh ginger

1 Tbsp. loosely packed orange zest
5 oranges, peeled and sectioned

1. Combine first 3 ingredients in a small saucepan; cover and cook over medium heat 2 minutes. Uncover and cook, stirring constantly, 3 more minutes or until cranberry skins begin to split. Remove from heat, and stir in orange zest. Cool 15 minutes.

2. Stir in orange sections, and chill 8 hours. **Makes 2½ cups.**

BLACKBERRY JAM CAKE

(pictured on page 159)

*An entire jar of blackberry jam and a generous helping of spice give
this pound cake vibrant flavor, even when blackberries are out of season.*

makes 12 servings   hands-on 30 min.   total 3 hours, 45 min.

1	cup buttermilk		1½	tsp. ground cinnamon
1	tsp. baking soda		1	tsp. ground allspice
1	cup butter, softened		¾	tsp. ground cloves
2	cups granulated sugar		½	tsp. table salt
4	large eggs, at room temperature		1	(18-oz.) jar seedless blackberry jam
1	tsp. vanilla extract		1	cup toasted finely chopped pecans
3	cups all-purpose flour			Powdered sugar (optional)

1. Preheat oven to 350°. Stir together buttermilk and baking soda.

2. Beat butter at medium speed with an electric mixer until creamy. Gradually add granulated sugar, beating until light and fluffy and stopping to scrape bowl as needed. Add eggs, 1 at a time, beating just until blended after each addition. Beat in vanilla.

3. Stir together flour and next 4 ingredients in a large bowl; gradually add to butter mixture alternately with buttermilk mixture, beginning and ending with flour mixture. Beat at low speed just until blended after each addition, stopping to scrape bowl as needed. Add jam, and beat at low speed just until blended. Stir in pecans. Spoon batter into a greased and floured 10-inch (14-cup) Bundt pan.

4. Bake at 350° for 1 hour and 5 minutes to 1 hour and 10 minutes or until a long wooden pick inserted in center comes out clean. Cool in pan on a wire rack 10 minutes; remove from pan to wire rack, and cool completely (about 2 hours). Dust cake with powdered sugar, if desired.

✕✕✕✕✕✕✕✕✕✕✕✕✕✕✕✕✕✕✕✕✕✕✕✕✕✕✕✕✕✕✕

sweet idea

This humble pound cake can be made into a stunning
centerpiece by baking the batter in an ornate Bundt pan,
lightly dusting with powdered sugar, and displaying on a tall
cake stand. While some batters can be crumbly or uneven,
this recipe is ideal for the more intricately decorated Bundt pans.

✕✕✕✕✕✕✕✕✕✕✕✕✕✕✕✕✕✕✕✕✕✕✕✕✕✕✕✕✕✕✕✕✕

LEMON-LIME POUND CAKE

(pictured on page 159)

*This recipe is based on a classic Southern favorite called 7UP Pound Cake,
which was created in the 1950s when the soda company suggested
using its soft drink instead of other liquid in pound cake recipes.
The result: one of the best, and simplest, cakes you'll ever make.*

makes 12 servings   hands-on 20 min.   total 1 hour, 35 min.

1½ cups butter, softened	1 tsp. lemon extract
3 cups sugar	3 cups all-purpose flour
5 large eggs	1 cup lemon-lime soft drink (such as 7UP)
2 Tbsp. lemon zest	Shortening
1 tsp. vanilla extract	Lemon-Lime Glaze

1. Preheat oven to 350°. Beat butter at medium speed with a heavy-duty electric stand mixer until creamy. Gradually add sugar; beat at medium speed 3 to 5 minutes or until light and fluffy. Add eggs, 1 at a time, beating just until blended after each addition. Stir in lemon zest and extracts.

2. Add flour to butter mixture alternately with lemon-lime soft drink, beginning and ending with flour. Beat at low speed just until blended after each addition. Pour batter into a greased (with shortening) and floured 10-inch (12-cup) Bundt pan.

3. Bake at 350° for 1 hour and 5 minutes to 1 hour and 15 minutes or until a long wooden pick inserted in center comes out clean, shielding with aluminum foil after 45 to 50 minutes to prevent excessive browning. Cool in pan on a wire rack 10 minutes; remove cake from pan to wire rack.

4. Spoon Lemon-Lime Glaze over warm or room temperature cake.

LEMON-LIME GLAZE

2 cups powdered sugar	1 Tbsp. fresh lime juice
2 tsp. firmly packed lemon zest	1 Tbsp. fresh lemon juice (optional)
1½ Tbsp. fresh lemon juice	

Whisk together powdered sugar, lemon zest, 1½ Tbsp. fresh lemon juice, and lime juice in a bowl until blended and smooth. (For a thinner glaze, stir in an additional 1 Tbsp. fresh lemon juice, 1 tsp. at a time, if desired.) **Makes about 1 cup.**

MINI APPLE CIDER POUND CAKES

Finish the cakes with one of the three toppings. Toss together the Streusel Topping before you start baking. Both glazes can be prepped while the cakes cool.

makes 6 mini loaves   hands-on 30 min.   total 2 hours, 20 min.

1½ cups butter, softened
3 cups sugar
6 large eggs
3 cups all-purpose flour
1 tsp. apple pie spice
½ tsp. baking powder
¼ tsp. table salt
¼ tsp. ground cloves

1 cup apple cider
1 tsp. vanilla extract
6 (5- x 3-inch) disposable aluminum foil pans
Vegetable cooking spray
Streusel Topping
Bourbon Glaze
Lemon Icing (page 101)

1. Preheat oven to 325°. Beat butter at medium speed with a heavy-duty electric stand mixer until creamy; gradually add sugar, beating until light and fluffy. Add eggs, 1 at a time, beating just until blended after each addition.

2. Stir together flour and next 4 ingredients. Gradually add flour mixture to butter mixture alternately with apple cider, beginning and ending with flour mixture. Beat at low speed just until blended after each addition. Stir in vanilla.

3. Lightly grease disposable loaf pans with cooking spray. Pour batter into prepared pans, and place on a baking sheet. For streusel-topped cakes, sprinkle about 2 Tbsp. Streusel Topping over batter in each pan.

4. Bake at 325° for 40 to 50 minutes or until a wooden pick inserted in center comes out clean. Cool in pans on wire racks 10 minutes; remove from pans to wire racks, and cool completely (about 1 hour). For glaze-topped cakes, spoon desired glaze over cooled cakes.

STREUSEL TOPPING

¾ cup all-purpose flour
½ cup chopped pecans
¼ cup butter, melted

2 Tbsp. sugar
1 tsp. apple pie spice
⅛ tsp. table salt

Stir together flour, pecans, melted butter, sugar, apple pie spice, and salt. Let stand 30 minutes or until firm. Crumble into small pieces. **Makes about 1 cup.**

BOURBON GLAZE

2 cups powdered sugar
1 Tbsp. bourbon

3 to 4 Tbsp. milk

Stir together powdered sugar, bourbon, and milk. **Makes about 1 cup.**

APPLE-CREAM CHEESE BUNDT CAKE

This delicious apple Bundt cake features a sweet cream cheese filling and homemade praline frosting. To dress it up even more, garnish the frosting with extra toasted pecans.

makes 12 servings   hands-on 40 min.   total 4 hours, 10 min.

Cream Cheese Filling:
1   (8-oz.) package cream cheese, softened
¼   cup butter, softened
½   cup granulated sugar
1   large egg
2   Tbsp. all-purpose flour
1   tsp. vanilla extract

Apple Cake Batter:
3   cups all-purpose flour
1   cup granulated sugar
1   cup firmly packed light brown sugar
2   tsp. ground cinnamon

1   tsp. table salt
1   tsp. baking soda
1   tsp. ground nutmeg
½   tsp. ground allspice
3   large eggs, lightly beaten
¾   cup canola oil
¾   cup applesauce
1   tsp. vanilla extract
3   cups peeled and finely chopped
     Gala apples (about 1½ lb.)
1   cup toasted finely chopped pecans
Praline Frosting

1. Prepare Cream Cheese Filling: Beat first 3 ingredients at medium speed with an electric mixer until blended and smooth. Add egg, flour, and vanilla; beat just until blended.

2. Prepare Apple Cake Batter: Preheat oven to 350°. Stir together 3 cups flour and next 7 ingredients in a large bowl; stir in eggs and next 3 ingredients, stirring just until dry ingredients are moistened. Stir in apples and pecans.

3. Spoon two-thirds of apple mixture into a greased and floured 10-inch (14-cup) Bundt pan. Spoon Cream Cheese Filling over apple mixture, leaving a 1-inch border around edges of pan. Swirl filling gently with a knife. Spoon remaining apple mixture over Cream Cheese Filling.

4. Bake at 350° for 1 hour to 1 hour and 15 minutes or until a long wooden pick inserted in center comes out clean. Cool cake in pan on a wire rack 15 minutes; remove from pan to wire rack, and cool completely (about 2 hours).

5. Pour frosting immediately over cooled cake.

PRALINE FROSTING

½   cup firmly packed light brown sugar
¼   cup butter
3   Tbsp. milk

1   tsp. vanilla extract
1   cup powdered sugar

Bring ½ cup brown sugar, ¼ cup butter, and 3 Tbsp. milk to a boil in a 2-qt. saucepan over medium heat, whisking constantly; boil 1 minute, whisking constantly. Remove from heat; stir in vanilla. Gradually whisk in powdered sugar until smooth; stir gently 3 to 5 minutes or until mixture begins to cool and thickens slightly. Use immediately. **Makes about 1 cup.**

pecans

One of the iconic ingredients on the Southern dessert table is the pecan. While the nuts are good for eating alone, pecans are most prized for their contribution to cakes, pies, and cookies, as well as to many meat and vegetable dishes. A member of the hickory family, the pecan tree is the only major nut tree native to the U.S. Today, Georgia is the country's top producer of pecans, and Albany, Georgia—home to more than 600,000 pecan trees—is the official pecan capital of the world.

COCONUT-ALMOND ROULADE

*Light and ethereal with a whipped coconut cream frosting,
this roulade is a showstopper at celebrations year-round. Roll up the
cake gently as to not squeeze out any of the luxurious frosting.*

makes 8 to 10 servings   hands-on 50 min.   total 3 hours

Cake:
Vegetable cooking spray
Parchment paper
3   large eggs
3   large egg yolks
¾   cup granulated sugar
½   cup coconut milk
3   Tbsp. butter, melted
1   tsp. almond extract
¾   cup cake flour
½   cup powdered sugar

Frosting:
2   cups heavy cream
½   cup coconut milk
½   cup powdered sugar
¼   tsp. table salt

Remaining ingredients:
½   cup sweetened flaked coconut
Toasted coconut flakes and toasted
    sliced almonds

1. Prepare Cake: Preheat oven to 400°. Lightly grease an 18- x 13-inch jelly-roll pan with cooking spray, and line with parchment paper. Spray parchment paper, and dust with cake flour, tapping out excess.

2. Beat eggs, egg yolks, and ¾ cup granulated sugar at high speed with an electric mixer 5 minutes or until thick and pale.

3. Stir together coconut milk and next 2 ingredients in a small bowl. Gently fold coconut milk mixture into egg mixture. Sift ¾ cup cake flour into mixture, ¼ cup at a time, folding until blended after each addition. Spread batter in prepared pan.

4. Bake at 400° for 10 to 12 minutes or until puffed. Cool in pan on a wire rack 10 minutes. Sprinkle ½ cup powdered sugar over top of cake. Invert cake onto a parchment paper-lined surface. Peel top layer of parchment paper from cake. Starting at 1 short side, roll up cake and bottom parchment together. Cool completely.

5. Prepare Frosting: Beat cream and coconut milk at medium speed until blended. Gradually add ½ cup powdered sugar and salt, whisking until stiff peaks form. Chill 1½ cups frosting.

6. Assemble: Unroll cake onto a flat surface. Spread with remaining frosting, leaving a 1-inch border on all sides. Sprinkle ½ cup coconut over frosting. Lift and tilt parchment paper, and roll up cake, jelly-roll fashion, starting at 1 short side and using parchment paper as a guide. Place cake, wrapped in parchment paper, on a baking sheet. Freeze 30 minutes to 24 hours. Let stand at room temperature 1 hour before serving. Remove parchment and top with chilled frosting and toasted coconut and almonds. Serve immediately.

STRAWBERRIES-AND-CREAM SHEET CAKE

*Trust us: This simple and swoon-worthy sheet cake will be a keeper
in your recipe box. File it under "Springtime Crowd-pleaser."*

makes 10 to 12 servings   hands-on 35 min.   total 2 hours, 50 min., including frosting

1   cup butter, softened
2   cups sugar
2   large eggs
2   tsp. fresh lemon juice
1   tsp. vanilla extract
2½ cups cake flour
2   Tbsp. strawberry-flavored gelatin
½ tsp. baking soda

¼ tsp. table salt
1   cup buttermilk
⅔ cup chopped fresh strawberries
Shortening
Parchment paper
Vegetable cooking spray
Strawberry Frosting
Garnish: fresh strawberries

1. Preheat oven to 350°. Beat butter at medium speed with an electric mixer until creamy; gradually add sugar, beating 4 to 5 minutes or until light and fluffy. Add eggs, 1 at a time, beating until blended after each addition. Beat in lemon juice and vanilla.

2. Stir together flour and next 3 ingredients; add flour mixture to butter mixture alternately with buttermilk, beginning and ending with flour mixture. Beat at low speed just until blended. Stir in chopped strawberries.

3. Grease (with shortening) and flour a 13- x 9-inch pan; line with parchment paper, allowing 2 to 3 inches to extend over long sides. Lightly grease paper with cooking spray. Spread batter in prepared pan.

4. Bake at 350° for 30 to 40 minutes or until a wooden pick inserted in center comes out clean. Cool in pan on a wire rack 30 minutes. Lift cake from pan, using parchment paper sides as handles. Invert cake onto wire rack; gently remove parchment paper. Cool completely (about 1 hour). Spread Strawberry Frosting on top and sides of cake.

STRAWBERRY FROSTING

1   (8-oz.) package cream cheese, softened
⅔ cup sugar, divided
⅔ cup chopped fresh strawberries

1   drop pink food coloring gel (optional)
1½ cups heavy cream
2   Tbsp. fresh lemon juice

1. Beat cream cheese and ⅓ cup sugar at medium speed with an electric mixer until smooth. Add strawberries and food coloring (if desired); beat until blended.

2. Beat cream and juice at medium speed until foamy; increase speed to medium-high, and slowly add remaining ⅓ cup sugar, beating until stiff peaks form. Fold half of cream mixture into cheese mixture; fold in remaining cream mixture. Use immediately. **Makes about 5 cups.**

SWEET TEA~AND~ LEMONADE CAKE

*Feeling rowdy? Spin this into a tipsy cake by substituting up to
2 Tbsp. vodka or bourbon for the lemon juice in the frosting.*

makes 12 to 15 servings   hands-on 35 min.   total 2 hours, 15 min., including frosting

Shortening
1½ cups boiling water
3   family-size tea bags
1   cup butter, softened
2   cups granulated sugar
½   cup firmly packed light brown sugar
5   large eggs, at room temperature

3½ cups cake flour
2   tsp. baking powder
¾   tsp. table salt
¼   tsp. baking soda
Lemonade Frosting
Garnish: lemon slices

1. Preheat oven to 350°. Grease (with shortening) and flour a 13- x 9-inch pan. Pour 1½ cups boiling water over tea bags in a heatproof glass bowl. Cover with plastic wrap, and steep 10 minutes. Lift tea bags from liquid, and press against side of bowl, using back of a spoon; discard tea bags. Cool tea 20 minutes.

2. Beat butter in a separate large bowl at medium speed with an electric mixer until creamy. Gradually add sugars, beating until light and fluffy. Add eggs, 1 at a time, beating just until blended after each addition. Whisk together cake flour and next 3 ingredients; add to butter mixture alternately with 1 cup tea, beginning and ending with flour mixture. (Discard any remaining tea.) Beat at low speed just until blended after each addition. Pour batter into prepared pan.

3. Bake at 350° for 35 to 40 minutes or until a wooden pick inserted in center comes out clean. Cool completely on a wire rack (about 20 minutes). Spread Lemonade Frosting on cake.
Note: We tested with Luzianne Iced Tea Bags.

LEMONADE FROSTING

1   (8-oz.) package cream cheese, softened
¼   cup butter, softened
6   cups powdered sugar

1   Tbsp. firmly packed lemon zest
3   Tbsp. fresh lemon juice

Beat cream cheese and butter at medium speed with an electric mixer until creamy. Gradually add powdered sugar, 1 cup at a time, beating at low speed until blended after each addition. Beat in lemon zest and lemon juice just until blended. Increase speed to high, and beat until light and fluffy. **Makes about 4 cups.**

~ strawberries ~

You know spring is here when you take that first bite into a plump, juicy strawberry. Enjoy the freshest berries while you can—the season peaks in May. Whether picked by hand at a local farm or bought from the grocery, choose brightly colored berries that still have their green caps attached. If fully ripe, they should have a potent strawberry fragrance.

STRAWBERRY~LEMONADE LAYER CAKE

You can assemble this glorious cake up to two days ahead; store at room temperature.
Also, you can freeze cooled layers up to a month in plastic wrap and aluminum foil.

makes 12 servings   hands-on 45 min.   total 4 hours, 30 min., including jam and frosting

1 cup butter, softened	1 cup milk
2 cups granulated sugar	1 Tbsp. loosely packed lemon zest
4 large eggs, separated	1 Tbsp. fresh lemon juice
3 cups cake flour	Shortening
1 Tbsp. baking powder	Strawberry-Lemonade Jam
⅛ tsp. table salt	Strawberry Frosting (page 170)

1. Preheat oven to 350°. Beat butter at medium speed with an electric mixer until creamy; gradually add sugar, beating until light and fluffy. Add egg yolks, 1 at a time, beating until blended after each addition.

2. Stir together flour and next 2 ingredients; add to butter mixture alternately with milk, beginning and ending with flour mixture. Beat at low speed just until blended. Stir in zest and juice.

3. Beat egg whites in a large bowl at high speed until stiff peaks form. Gently stir one-third of egg whites into batter; fold in remaining egg whites. Spoon batter into 4 greased (with shortening) and floured 9-inch round cake pans.

4. Bake at 350° for 16 to 20 minutes or until a wooden pick inserted in center comes out clean. Cool in pans on wire racks 10 minutes; remove from pans to wire racks, and cool completely.

5. Place 1 cake layer on a serving platter, and spread with about ½ cup Strawberry-Lemonade Jam, leaving a ½-inch border around edges. Spoon 1 cup Strawberry Frosting into a zip-top plastic freezer bag. Snip 1 corner of bag to make a small hole. Pipe a ring of frosting around cake layer just inside the top edge. Top with second and third cake layers, repeating procedure with filling and frosting between each layer. Top with last cake layer, and spread remaining Strawberry Frosting on top and sides of cake.

STRAWBERRY~LEMONADE JAM

2½ cups chopped fresh strawberries	¼ cup fresh lemon juice
¾ cup sugar	3 Tbsp. cornstarch

1. Process strawberries in a blender until smooth; press through a wire-mesh strainer into a 3-qt. saucepan, using back of a spoon to squeeze out juice; discard pulp. Stir in sugar.

2. Whisk together lemon juice and cornstarch; gradually whisk into strawberry mixture. Bring mixture to a boil over medium heat, and cook, whisking constantly, 1 minute. Remove from heat. Place plastic wrap directly on warm jam; chill 2 hours or until cold. Refrigerate in an airtight container up to 1 week. **Makes about 1⅔ cups.**

CHOCOLATE VELVET CAKE WITH COCONUT~PECAN FROSTING

*We've updated this classic cake with deep chocolate
layers and a rich filling that doubles as a frosting.*

makes 12 servings   hands-on 25 min.   total 1 hour, 40 min., including frosting

1½ cups semisweet chocolate morsels
½ cup butter, softened
1 (16-oz.) package light brown sugar
3 large eggs
2 cups all-purpose flour
1 tsp. baking soda

½ tsp. table salt
1 (8-oz.) container sour cream
1 cup hot water
2 tsp. vanilla extract
Coconut-Pecan Frosting

1. Preheat oven to 350°. Microwave chocolate in a microwave-safe bowl at HIGH 1 to 1½ minutes or until melted and smooth, stirring at 30-second intervals. Beat butter and brown sugar at medium speed with an electric mixer until well blended (about 5 minutes). Add eggs, 1 at a time, beating just until blended after each addition. Add melted chocolate, beating just until blended.

2. Sift together flour, baking soda, and salt. Gradually add to chocolate mixture alternately with sour cream, beginning and ending with flour mixture. Beat at low speed just until blended after each addition. Gradually add 1 cup hot water in a slow, steady stream, beating at low speed just until blended. Stir in vanilla.

3. Spoon batter evenly into 3 greased and floured 9-inch round cake pans. Bake at 350° for 25 to 30 minutes or until a wooden pick inserted in center comes out clean. Cool in pans on a wire rack 10 minutes. Remove from pans, and let cool completely on wire rack.

4. Spread Coconut-Pecan Frosting between layers and on top of cake.

COCONUT~PECAN FROSTING

1 (12-oz.) can evaporated milk
1½ cups sugar
¾ cup butter
6 large egg yolks

2 cups toasted chopped pecans
1½ cups sweetened flaked coconut
1½ tsp. vanilla extract

Stir together first 4 ingredients in a heavy 3-qt. saucepan over medium heat; bring to a boil, and cook, stirring constantly, 12 minutes. Remove from heat; add remaining ingredients, and stir until frosting is cool and spreading consistency. **Makes about 5 cups.**

LEMON~ORANGE CHIFFON CAKE

Light-as-air with a spongy texture, chiffon cakes are the kind of dessert that's welcomed even on a hot day or after a rich meal. With fresh lemons and oranges to flavor the cake and frosting, this dessert will have your guests clamoring for a slice, and the recipe to go with it.

makes 12 servings   hands-on 30 min.   total 2 hours, 10 min.

2½ cups sifted cake flour
1⅓ cups sugar
1 Tbsp. baking powder
1 tsp. table salt
½ cup vegetable oil
5 large eggs, separated

3 Tbsp. loosely packed orange zest
¾ cup fresh orange juice
½ tsp. cream of tartar
Lemon-Orange Buttercream Frosting
Garnishes: fresh mint leaves, lemon or orange slices

1. Preheat oven to 350°. Combine first 4 ingredients in bowl of a heavy-duty electric stand mixer. Make a well in center of flour mixture; add oil, egg yolks, and orange juice. Beat at medium-high speed 3 to 4 minutes or until smooth. Stir in zest.

2. Beat egg whites and cream of tartar at medium-high speed until stiff peaks form. Gently fold into flour mixture. Spoon batter into 3 greased and floured 9-inch round cake pans.

3. Bake at 350° for 17 to 20 minutes or until a wooden pick inserted in center comes out clean. Cool in pans on wire racks 10 minutes; remove from pans to wire racks, and cool completely (about 1 hour).

4. Spread Lemon-Orange Buttercream Frosting between layers and on top and sides of cake.

LEMON~ORANGE BUTTERCREAM FROSTING

1 cup butter, softened
3 Tbsp. orange zest, loosely packed
1 Tbsp. lemon zest, loosely packed
1 (32-oz.) package powdered sugar

3 Tbsp. fresh lemon juice
5 Tbsp. fresh orange juice
1 Tbsp. fresh orange juice

Beat butter, orange zest, and lemon zest at medium speed with an electric mixer 1 to 2 minutes or until creamy; gradually add powdered sugar alternately with 3 Tbsp. lemon juice and 5 Tbsp. fresh orange juice, beating at low speed until blended after each addition. Add up to 1 Tbsp. fresh orange juice, 1 tsp. at a time, until spreading consistency. **Makes about 6 cups.**

Tip: This recipe calls for sifted cake flour, so be sure to sift it before measuring. If you don't, you'll be using too much flour and you won't get the lightness of a chiffon cake.

FLOURLESS CHOCOLATE TORTE

*Experience the decadence of chocolate in this rich, fudgy cake.
The intense chocolate flavor comes from both cocoa and semisweet
chocolate squares. If you're looking for a gluten-free cake to make
without buying any specialty ingredients, this is the perfect choice.*

makes 8 servings   hands-on 25 min.   total 1 hour

Unsweetened cocoa
2 (8-oz.) packages semisweet chocolate
   baking squares, coarsely chopped
½ cup butter

5 large eggs, separated
1 Tbsp. vanilla extract
¼ cup sugar

1. Preheat oven to 375°. Grease a 9-inch springform pan, and dust with unsweetened cocoa; set aside.

2. Melt chopped chocolate and butter in a heavy saucepan over low heat, stirring constantly until smooth.

3. Whisk together egg yolks and vanilla in a large bowl. Gradually stir in chocolate mixture; whisk until well blended.

4. Beat egg whites at high speed with an electric mixer until soft peaks form. Gradually add sugar, beating until stiff peaks form and sugar dissolves (about 2 to 4 minutes). Fold one-third beaten egg white mixture into chocolate mixture; gently fold in remaining egg white mixture just until blended. Spoon batter into prepared pan, spreading evenly.

5. Bake at 375° for 25 minutes. (Do not overbake.) Let stand in pan on a wire rack 10 minutes before removing sides of pan.

×××××××××××××××××××××××××××××××××××

sweet idea

Serve this decadent cake while it's warm topped
with a scattering of fresh raspberries and
a small bowl of crème fraîche; the tangy cream
complements the richness of the intense chocolate.

×××××××××××××××××××××××××××××××××××

Sweet Potato Coffee Cake
with Caramel Glaze

Chocolate-Cream
Cheese Coffee Cake

Caramel Apple
Coffee Cake

Honey-Pineapple
Upside-Down Cake

SWEET POTATO COFFEE CAKE

(pictured on page 182)

makes 2 (10-inch cakes)   hands-on 30 min.   total 3 hours, 15 min., including glaze

2 (¼-oz.) envelopes active dry yeast	½ cup granulated sugar
½ cup warm water (100° to 110°)	¼ cup butter, melted
1 tsp. granulated sugar	1 Tbsp. loosely packed orange zest
5½ cups bread flour	⅔ cup granulated sugar
1½ tsp. table salt	⅔ cup firmly packed brown sugar
1 tsp. baking soda	1 Tbsp. ground cinnamon
1 cup mashed cooked sweet potato	¼ cup butter, melted
1 large egg, lightly beaten	Caramel Glaze
1 cup buttermilk	

1. Stir together first 3 ingredients in a 1-cup glass measuring cup; let stand 5 minutes.

2. Stir together 4½ cups bread flour, salt, and baking soda. Beat yeast mixture and ½ cup bread flour at medium speed with a heavy-duty electric stand mixer until well blended. Gradually add sweet potato, next 5 ingredients, and flour mixture, beating until well blended. Turn dough out onto a well-floured surface, and knead until smooth and elastic, gradually adding ½ cup bread flour. Place dough in a lightly greased large bowl, turning to grease top. Cover and let rise in a warm place (80° to 85°), free from drafts, 1 hour or until doubled in bulk.

3. Stir together ⅔ cup granulated sugar and next 2 ingredients. Punch dough down; turn out onto a well-floured surface. Divide dough in half. Roll 1 portion into a 16- x 12-inch rectangle. Brush with half of ¼ cup melted butter. Sprinkle with half of sugar mixture. Cut dough lengthwise into 6 (2-inch-wide) strips using a pizza cutter or knife.

4. Loosely coil 1 strip (sugared side facing inward), and place in center of a lightly greased 10-inch round pan. Loosely coil remaining dough strips, 1 at a time, around center strip to make a single large spiral. Repeat with remaining dough half, butter, and sugar mixture. Cover and let rise in a warm place (80° to 85°), free from drafts, 30 minutes or until doubled in bulk.

5. Preheat oven to 350°. Bake at 350° for 30 minutes or until lightly browned. Cool in pans on a wire rack 10 minutes. Remove from pans to serving plates. Brush Caramel Glaze over swirls.

CARAMEL GLAZE

1 cup firmly packed brown sugar	1 cup powdered sugar, sifted
½ cup butter	1 tsp. vanilla extract
¼ cup evaporated milk	

Bring first 3 ingredients to a boil over medium heat, whisking constantly. Boil, whisking constantly, 1 minute. Remove from heat; whisk in powdered sugar and vanilla until smooth. Stir gently 3 to 5 minutes or until mixture begins to cool and thicken. Use immediately. **Makes about 1½ cups.**

CHOCOLATE~CREAM CHEESE COFFEE CAKE

(pictured on page 182)

A swirl of cream cheese is the perfect contrast against the intense chocolate in this treat.

makes 2 (9-inch) cakes   hands-on 35 min.   total 1 hour, 20 min.

Crumble Topping:
1⅓ cups all-purpose flour
½ cup firmly packed brown sugar
½ cup cold butter, cut up
1 cup chopped pecans

Cream Cheese Batter:
1 (8-oz.) package cream cheese, softened
¼ cup granulated sugar
1 Tbsp. all-purpose flour
1 large egg
½ tsp. vanilla extract

Chocolate Velvet Cake Batter:
1½ cups semisweet chocolate morsels
½ cup butter, softened

1 (16-oz.) package light brown sugar
3 large eggs
2 cups all-purpose flour
1 tsp. baking soda
½ tsp. table salt
1 (8-oz.) container sour cream
1 cup hot water
2 tsp. vanilla extract

Vanilla Glaze:
1 cup powdered sugar
2 Tbsp. milk
½ tsp. vanilla extract

1. Prepare Crumble Topping: Preheat oven to 350°. Stir together 1⅓ cups flour and brown sugar in a medium bowl. Cut butter into flour mixture with pastry blender or fork until crumbly; stir in pecans; set aside.

2. Prepare Cream Cheese Batter: Beat cream cheese at medium speed with an electric mixer until smooth; add granulated sugar and 1 Tbsp. flour, beating until blended. Add egg and ½ tsp. vanilla, beating until blended; set aside.

3. Prepare Chocolate Velvet Cake Batter: Microwave chocolate in a microwave-safe bowl at HIGH 1 to 1½ minutes or until melted and smooth, stirring at 30-second intervals. Beat butter and brown sugar at medium speed with an electric mixer until well blended. Add eggs, 1 at a time, beating just until blended after each addition. Add melted chocolate, beating just until blended. Sift together flour, baking soda, and salt. Gradually add to chocolate mixture alternately with sour cream, beginning and ending with flour mixture. Beat at low speed just until blended after each addition. Gradually add 1 cup hot water in a slow, steady stream, beating at low speed just until blended. Stir in vanilla.

4. Spoon Chocolate Velvet Cake Batter evenly into 2 greased and floured 9-inch springform pans. Dollop cream cheese mixture evenly over cake batter, and swirl batter gently with a knife. Sprinkle reserved pecan mixture evenly over cake batter.

5. Bake at 350° for 45 minutes or until set. Cool on a wire rack.

6. Prepare Vanilla Glaze: Whisk together powdered sugar, milk, and ½ tsp. vanilla. Drizzle evenly over tops of coffee cakes.

CARAMEL APPLE COFFEE CAKE

(pictured on page 183)

Autumn flavor abounds with apple slices, cinnamon, and pecans in this coffee cake.

makes 8 to 10 servings   hands-on 35 min.   total 4 hours, 50 min., including sauce

2   Tbsp. butter
3   cups peeled and sliced Granny Smith
    apples (about 3 large)
Caramel Sauce
3½ cups all-purpose flour, divided
1   cup chopped pecans
½   cup butter, melted
½   cup firmly packed light brown sugar

1¼ cups granulated sugar, divided
1½ tsp. ground cinnamon
¾   tsp. table salt, divided
½   cup butter, softened
2   large eggs
2   tsp. baking powder
⅔   cup milk
2   tsp. vanilla extract

1. Preheat oven to 350°. Melt 2 Tbsp. butter in a large skillet over medium-high heat; add apples, and sauté 5 minutes or until softened. Remove from heat; cool completely (about 30 minutes).

2. Meanwhile, prepare Caramel Sauce. Reserve ½ cup Caramel Sauce for another use.

3. In a medium bowl, stir together 1½ cups flour, pecans, melted butter, brown sugar, ¼ cup granulated sugar, cinnamon, and ¼ tsp. salt until blended; set aside.

4. Beat ½ cup softened butter at medium speed with an electric mixer until creamy; gradually add remaining 1 cup sugar, beating well. Add eggs, 1 at a time, beating until blended after each addition.

5. Combine remaining 2 cups flour, baking powder, and remaining ½ tsp. salt; add to butter mixture alternately with milk, beginning and ending with flour mixture. Beat at low speed until blended after each addition. Stir in vanilla. Pour batter into a greased and floured shiny 9-inch springform pan; top with apples. Drizzle with ½ cup Caramel Sauce; sprinkle with streusel topping.

6. Bake at 350° for 45 minutes. Cover loosely with aluminum foil to prevent excessive browning; bake 25 to 30 minutes or until center is set. (A wooden pick will not come out clean.) Cool in pan on a wire rack 30 minutes; remove sides of pan. Cool completely on wire rack (about 1½ hours). Drizzle with ½ cup Caramel Sauce.

CARAMEL SAUCE

1   cup firmly packed light brown sugar
½   cup butter

¼   cup whipping cream
¼   cup honey

Bring brown sugar, butter, whipping cream, and honey to a boil in a medium saucepan over medium-high heat, stirring constantly; boil, stirring constantly, 2 minutes. Remove from heat, and cool 15 minutes before serving. Store in an airtight container in refrigerator up to 1 week. **Makes about 1½ cups.**

HONEY-PINEAPPLE UPSIDE-DOWN CAKE

(pictured on page 183)

Instead of the traditional brown sugar, pineapples get tucked into a swirl of honey in the skillet before the batter. Just in case you didn't get enough of this sweet nectar, turn out the cake onto a rimmed platter and pour on the Honey Glaze.

makes 10 to 12 servings   hands-on 20 min.   total 1 hour, 45 min.

⅔ cup honey
Butter
1 (20-oz.) can pineapple slices in juice, drained*
1⅓ cups sugar
¾ cup butter, softened
1 tsp. vanilla extract
1¾ cups all-purpose flour

¼ cup plain yellow cornmeal
1 tsp. baking powder
1 tsp. table salt
½ tsp. baking soda
¾ cup buttermilk
3 large eggs
Honey Glaze

1. Preheat oven to 350°. Pour honey into a buttered 10-inch cast-iron skillet, tilting skillet to spread evenly. Top with pineapple.

2. Beat sugar and ¾ cup butter at medium speed with a heavy-duty electric stand mixer until fluffy. Stir in vanilla. Whisk together flour and next 4 ingredients. Whisk together buttermilk and eggs. Add flour mixture to sugar mixture alternately with buttermilk mixture, beginning and ending with flour mixture. Beat just until blended. Spread batter over pineapple.

3. Bake at 350° for 50 minutes or until a wooden pick inserted in center comes out clean, shielding with aluminum foil after 45 minutes to prevent excessive browning, if necessary. Cool in skillet on a wire rack 10 minutes.

4. Invert cake onto a serving platter. Drizzle with Honey Glaze. Let cool 15 minutes before serving.

*Fresh pineapple slices work well here too.

HONEY GLAZE

¼ cup honey
1 Tbsp. light brown sugar

1 Tbsp. butter

Bring honey, brown sugar, and butter to a simmer in a small saucepan. Cook 1 minute. Makes about ⅓ cup.

BANANAS FOSTER COFFEE CAKE WITH VANILLA~RUM SAUCE

You don't have to wait for Mardi Gras to bake up this rum-infused cake from New Orleans. Banana slices are first sautéed in a buttery rum glaze then folded into a simple coffee cake batter and topped off with a crumble.

makes 8 to 10 servings   hands-on 20 min.   total 1 hour, 45 min.

1½ cups mashed ripe bananas
7   Tbsp. light rum, divided
2   cups firmly packed brown sugar, divided
1½ cups soft butter, divided
2   tsp. vanilla extract, divided
1   (8-oz.) package cream cheese, softened
2   large eggs
3¼ cups plus 3 Tbsp. all-purpose flour, divided

⅝   tsp. table salt, divided
½   tsp. baking powder
½   tsp. baking soda
1½ cups chopped pecans
1   tsp. ground cinnamon
1   cup granulated sugar
2   cups heavy cream

1. Preheat oven to 350°. Cook bananas, 3 Tbsp. rum, ½ cup brown sugar, and ¼ cup butter in a skillet until mixture is bubbly. Cool; stir in 1 tsp. vanilla.

2. Beat cream cheese and ½ cup butter at medium speed with an electric mixer until creamy. Add 1 cup brown sugar; beat until fluffy. Beat in eggs, 1 at a time.

3. Stir together 3 cups flour, ½ tsp. salt, and next 2 ingredients; add to cream cheese mixture. Beat at low speed until blended. Stir in banana mixture. Spoon into a greased and floured 13- x 9-inch pan.

4. Combine pecans, cinnamon, ½ cup brown sugar, and ¼ cup flour. Melt ¼ cup butter; stir into pecan mixture. Sprinkle over batter. Bake at 350° for 45 minutes or until a wooden pick inserted in center comes out clean. Cool in pan on a wire rack 10 minutes.

5. Combine granulated sugar, remaining 3 Tbsp. flour, and remaining ⅛ tsp. salt in a saucepan over medium heat. Add cream and remaining ½ cup butter; bring to a boil. Boil, whisking constantly, 2 minutes or until slightly thickened. Remove from heat; stir in remaining ¼ cup rum and remaining 1 tsp. vanilla. Drizzle over warm cake.

xxxxxxxxxxxxxxxxxxxxxxxxxxxxxxxxxxxxxx

time-saving tip

To make ahead, bake the coffee cake and make
the sauce a day ahead. Cool both, and cover.
Chill the sauce, and reheat just before serving.

xxxxxxxxxxxxxxxxxxxxxxxxxxxxxxxxxxxxxx

BLACKBERRY~PEACH COFFEE CAKE

Wait to make this recipe until you can get your hands on fresh and in-season peaches and blackberries—it is definitely worth it! If you've got a plethora of peaches to use up, follow the instructions below for the peach-only variation of this coffee cake.

makes 8 servings   hands-on 20 min.   total 3 hours, 10 min., including topping

Streusel Topping:
- ½ cup butter, softened
- ½ cup granulated sugar
- ½ cup firmly packed light brown sugar
- ⅔ cup all-purpose flour
- 1 tsp. ground cinnamon
- ½ tsp. ground nutmeg

Cake Batter:
- ½ cup butter, softened
- 1 cup granulated sugar
- 2 large eggs

- 2 cups all-purpose flour
- 2 tsp. baking powder
- ½ tsp. table salt
- ⅔ cup milk
- 2 tsp. vanilla extract
- 2 cups peeled and sliced fresh firm, ripe peaches (about 2 large peaches)
- 1 cup fresh blackberries
- Powdered sugar
- Garnishes: fresh blackberries, sliced peaches, whipped cream

1. Preheat oven to 350°. **Prepare Streusel Topping:** Beat butter at medium speed with an electric mixer until creamy; gradually add granulated sugar and brown sugar, beating well. Add flour, cinnamon, and nutmeg; beat just until blended; set aside.

2. Prepare Cake: Beat butter at medium speed with an electric mixer until creamy; gradually add granulated sugar, beating well. Add eggs, 1 at a time, beating until well blended after each addition.

3. Combine flour, baking powder, and salt; add to butter mixture alternately with milk, beginning and ending with flour mixture. Beat at low speed until blended after each addition. Stir in vanilla. Pour batter into a greased and floured 9-inch springform pan; top with sliced peaches and blackberries. Pinch off 1-inch pieces of Streusel Topping, and drop over fruit.

4. Bake at 350° for 1 hour and 10 minutes to 1 hour and 20 minutes or until center of cake is set. (A wooden pick inserted in center will not come out clean.) Cool completely on a wire rack (about 1½ hours). Dust with powdered sugar.

Tip: We found that using a shiny or light-colored pan gave us the best results. If you have a dark pan, wrap the outside of the pan with aluminum foil, shiny side out, to get a similar result.

Peach Coffee Cake: Omit blackberries. Increase peaches to 3 cups sliced (about 3 large peaches, 7 oz. each). Proceed with recipe as directed.

peaches

As summer rites of passage go, there is perhaps nothing more quintessentially Southern than pulling over at a roadside stand, handing over a few crinkled bills for a basket of farm-fresh peaches, and proceeding to take one big, satisfying bite of summer as juice trickles down your chin. In fact, we'll go out on a limb and declare the peach the unofficial fruit of the region. Sure, these juicy bombshells are embraced elsewhere, but where else do you hear people use phrases like "She's a real peach"? Where else do you pass water towers shaped like giant peaches? Where else can you find a reigning Peach Queen?

pies, tarts
& cobblers

PIECRUSTS

*Don't let piecrust dough intimidate you—all you need is a little practice
and a few pictures to guide you through the simple steps.*

The secret to a perfectly flaky crust is to obey two rules: Be gentle with the dough, and keep the ingredients and the dough cold. Once you master it, you will wonder why you ever doubted yourself. Before baking, give even the simplest pie a gorgeous fluted edge or lattice top for a showstopping look.

.......pastry blender dough.......

Step 1: Place flour and salt in a large bowl, mixing until combined.

Step 2: Add cold butter pieces and, using a pastry blender, combine until mixture resembles small peas.

Step 3: Sprinkle ice water, 1 Tbsp. at a time, over surface of mixture in bowl; stir with a fork until the dry ingredients are moistened.

Step 4: Continue mixing with a fork until ingredients just come together.

.......food processor dough.......

Step 1: Pulse flour and salt in a food processor 3 or 4 times or until just combined.

Step 2: Add cold butter pieces, and pulse 5 or 6 times or until crumbly.

Step 3: With food processor running, gradually add ice water, 1 Tbsp. at a time, and process until dough forms a ball and pulls away from sides of bowl, adding more water if necessary.

Step 4: Once the dough forms a ball, stop mixing so your crust will turn out tender and flaky.

......rolling & transferring......

Step 1: Form dough into a small disk, wrap in plastic wrap, and chill 30 minutes.

Step 2: Roll dough into a 13-inch circle on a lightly floured surface.

Step 3: Fold dough over rolling pin, and loosely roll onto pin.

Step 4: Unroll dough into pie plate, and gently press dough into plate.

......crimping & baking......

Step 1: Cut off excess dough, leaving 1-inch hangover all around. Turn edges under to align with edge of pie plate.

Step 2: Flute edges using the thumb and forefinger of one hand to form the dough around the thumb of the other.

Step 3: Line crust with parchment paper, and fill with pie weights or dried beans. Bake until edges are golden brown.

......creating pretty edges......

Fork Press: Press folded edges of crust with the tines of a fork. Repeat around crust edge.

Leafy Vine: Using kitchen shears, make ½-inch diagonal cuts around crust edge, ½ inch apart. Press every other tab toward center.

Lattice: Cut an additional piecrust into strips. Weave strips in a woven lattice design over filling; press ends to adhere.

Double Crust: Place an additional piecrust over filling. Fold edges under, sealing to bottom crust. Cut slits or cut out shapes to vent.

ROASTED CHERRY HAND PIES

Both savory and sweet hand pies are a Southern favorite most often deep fried. But vodka gives this baked version its tender flakiness. Roasting the cherries intensifies their flavor.

makes 1 dozen hand pies   hands-on 1 hour   total 4 hours, 55 min.

½ cup butter	6 Tbsp. Demerara sugar, divided
4 Tbsp. almond paste	½ cup dried cherries
2½ cups all-purpose flour	⅓ cup seedless raspberry preserves
¾ tsp. table salt	1 Tbsp. butter
¼ cup ice-cold vodka	1 tsp. vanilla bean paste
4 to 5 Tbsp. ice-cold water	Parchment paper
1 (12-oz.) package frozen sweet cherries	1 large egg

1. Cut ½ cup butter into small cubes; chill butter and almond paste 15 minutes. Stir together flour and salt. Cut butter and almond paste into flour mixture with a pastry blender until mixture resembles small peas. Gradually stir in vodka and ¼ cup ice-cold water with a fork, stirring just until dough begins to form a ball and leaves sides of bowl, adding up to 1 Tbsp. more water if necessary. Place dough on plastic wrap; shape into a flat disk.

2. Divide dough into 12 portions. Shape each into a ball. Flatten each into a 3-inch circle on a lightly floured surface; roll into a 5-inch circle. Stack circles between layers of plastic wrap or wax paper. Cover stack with plastic wrap; chill 2 to 24 hours.

3. Preheat oven to 425°. Spread frozen cherries in a lightly greased 13- x 9-inch baking dish; sprinkle with 4 Tbsp. Demerara sugar. Bake at 425° for 25 minutes or until juice begins to thicken, stirring every 10 minutes. Remove from oven; immediately scrape cherries and juice into a bowl, using a rubber spatula. Stir in dried cherries and next 3 ingredients; cover with plastic wrap. Cool completely (45 minutes).

4. Working with 1 circle at a time, spoon 1 heaping Tbsp. cherry mixture into center of each dough circle; fold dough over filling. Press edges together with a fork to seal. Place on a parchment paper-lined baking sheet. Whisk together egg and 1 Tbsp. water. Brush pies with egg mixture. Cut 1 to 2 slits in top of each pie; sprinkle with remaining Demerara sugar.

5. Bake at 425° for 15 to 20 minutes or until golden. Remove from pan to a wire rack, and cool 15 minutes.

xxxxxxxxxxxxxxxxxxxxxxxxxxxxxxxxxxxxxx

sweet idea

Wonderful fresh out of the oven or at room temperature, these hand-held treats lend themselves to dessert on the go. Gently pack them in a basket or tin to take on a picnic or a Sunday drive.

xxxxxxxxxxxxxxxxxxxxxxxxxxxxxxxxxxxxxx

SKILLET APPLE PIE

Cast-iron skillets are the workhorses of Southern kitchens for everything from cornbread to steak to desserts. For this easy dessert, simply toss together apples, cinnamon, and brown sugar, and spoon into a well-seasoned skillet, top with a piecrust, and bake.

makes 2 (6-inch) pies   hands-on 20 min.   total 1 hour, 40 min.

2   lb. Granny Smith apples
2   lb. Braeburn apples
1   tsp. ground cinnamon
¾   cup granulated sugar
2   recipes Simple Piecrust,
      prepared through Step 1 (page 214)

½   cup butter
1   cup firmly packed light brown sugar
1   large egg white
2   Tbsp. granulated sugar
Butter-pecan ice cream

1. Preheat oven to 350°. Peel apples, and cut into ½-inch-thick wedges. Toss apples with cinnamon and ¾ cup granulated sugar.

2. On a lightly floured surface, roll each round of Simple Piecrust to ¼-inch thickness. Using a 1½-inch fluted round cutter, cut 40 to 50 rounds from dough; cover and keep chilled.

3. Melt ¼ cup butter in each of 2 (6-inch) cast-iron skillets over medium heat; add ½ cup brown sugar to each pan, and cook, stirring constantly, 1 to 2 minutes or until sugar is dissolved. Remove from heat, and spoon apple mixture over syrup. Arrange half of dough cutouts over each pan of apples, overlapping edges. Whisk egg white until foamy. Brush top of piecrust with egg white; sprinkle with 2 Tbsp. granulated sugar.

4. Bake at 350° for 50 minutes to 1 hour or until golden brown and bubbly, shielding with aluminum foil during last 10 minutes to prevent excessive browning, if necessary. Cool on a wire rack 30 minutes before serving. Serve with butter-pecan ice cream.

Large Skillet Apple Pie: Prepare recipe as directed through Step 1. Roll each Simple Piecrust round to 1 (13-inch) circle. Melt butter in a 10-inch cast-iron skillet over medium heat; add brown sugar, and cook, stirring constantly, 1 to 2 minutes or until sugar is dissolved. Remove from heat, and place 1 piecrust in skillet over brown sugar mixture. Spoon apple mixture over piecrust, and top with remaining piecrust. Press edges together to adhere. Whisk egg white until foamy. Brush top of piecrust with egg white; sprinkle with 2 Tbsp. granulated sugar. Cut 4 or 5 slits in top for steam to escape. Continue with recipe as directed, increasing bake time to 1 hour to 1½ hours.

FRESH BLACKBERRY PIE

*For this Southern fruit pie, only the crust is baked, while the filling is cooked
on the stovetop and poured over the whole, fresh, summer berries.
While the food coloring can certainly be omitted, expect a more magenta-hued pie.*

makes 8 servings   hands-on 20 min.   total 10 hours, 50 min.

1½ cups fresh blackberries
1¼ cups sugar, divided
3   Tbsp. cornstarch
½   tsp. vanilla extract

1   (3-oz.) package raspberry gelatin
4   drops blue liquid food coloring (optional)
1   Simple Piecrust, baked (page 214)
Sweetened whipped cream (optional)

1. Gently toss berries and ¼ cup sugar in a large bowl; cover and chill 8 hours. Drain.

2. Stir together cornstarch and remaining 1 cup sugar in a small saucepan; slowly whisk in
1¼ cups water and vanilla. Cook over medium heat, whisking constantly, 7 to 8 minutes or
until mixture thickens.

3. Stir together raspberry gelatin and blue liquid food coloring, if desired, in a small bowl;
whisk into the warm cornstarch mixture.

4. Spoon blackberries into baked piecrust. Pour glaze evenly over berries, pressing down
gently with a spoon to be sure all berries are coated. Chill 2½ hours. Serve with whipped
cream, if desired.

xxxxxxxxxxxxxxxxxxxxxxxxxxxxxxxxxx

time-saving tip
Though this blackberry pie should be assembled and
served the same day, you can get a head start by combining
the berries and sugar and chilling them the night before.

xxxxxxxxxxxxxxxxxxxxxxxxxxxxxxxxxx

Pear-Cherry Pie
with Cheddar Crust

Individual
Berry Pies

Mile-High Mini
Strawberry Pies

Apple Slab Pie

PEAR~CHERRY PIE WITH CHEDDAR CRUST

(pictured on page 202)

*The savory goodness of Cheddar cheese gives this
crust a unique, out-of-this-world flakiness.*

makes 8 servings   hands-on 30 min.   total 3 hours, including piecrust

3¼ lb. Bartlett pears, peeled and sliced	1½ tsp. vanilla extract
1 cup dried cherries	1 tsp. chopped fresh rosemary
⅓ cup firmly packed light brown sugar	¼ tsp. table salt
¼ cup cornstarch	2 recipes Cheddar Piecrust Dough
1 Tbsp. granulated sugar	1 large egg, lightly beaten
2 Tbsp. fresh lemon juice	

1. Stir together pears and next 8 ingredients in a large bowl.

2. Preheat oven to 400°. Roll 1 dough disk into a 12½-inch circle on a lightly floured surface. Fit piecrust into a 10-inch pie plate; fold edges under, and crimp. Spoon pear mixture into crust.

3. Roll remaining dough disk to ⅛-inch thickness on a lightly floured surface, and cut into 6 (2½-inch) strips. Arrange strips in a lattice design over filling; press ends of strips into crust, sealing to bottom crust, and crimp. (Reroll scraps if you do not have enough strips to cover pie.) Whisk together egg and 2 Tbsp. water. Brush lattice with egg mixture.

4. Bake at 400° for 55 minutes to 1 hour, shielding with aluminum foil after 30 minutes to prevent excessive browning, if necessary. Let cool on a wire rack 1 hour.

CHEDDAR PIECRUST DOUGH

1¼ cups all-purpose flour	½ cup cold butter, cut into ½-inch cubes
1 Tbsp. sugar	1½ Tbsp. cold heavy cream
⅛ tsp. table salt	2 to 3 Tbsp. ice-cold water
½ cup finely grated sharp Cheddar cheese	

Pulse first 3 ingredients in a food processor 3 or 4 times or until combined. Add cheese and butter; pulse 10 to 12 times or until mixture resembles coarse meal. Drizzle cream and water over mixture; pulse 4 or 5 times or just until moist clumps form. Flatten dough into a disk; wrap in plastic wrap, and chill 30 minutes. **Makes 1 disk of dough (enough for 1 [9-inch] pie).**

MILE-HIGH MINI STRAWBERRY PIES

(pictured on page 203)

These little pies pack a punch of springtime flavor with their tart lemon filling and are a great way to utilize a bumper crop of farm stand or U-Pick strawberries.

makes 12 mini pies   hands-on 1 hour, 35 min.   total 6 hours, 30 min.

Crusts:
¼ cup powdered sugar
4 recipes Simple Piecrust, prepared
   through Step 1 (page 214)

Creamy Lemon Filling:
1½ (8-oz.) packages cream cheese,
   softened
1 Tbsp. sour cream
½ cup granulated sugar
2 tsp. loosely packed lemon zest
1 Tbsp. fresh lemon juice

Strawberry Topping:
1½ cups chopped fresh strawberries
1 cup granulated sugar
2 Tbsp. cornstarch
1 Tbsp. butter
10 cups hulled fresh strawberries

Vanilla Cream:
1 cup heavy cream
¼ tsp. vanilla extract
3 Tbsp. powdered sugar
Garnish: fresh mint leaves

1. Prepare Crusts: Preheat oven to 425°. Sprinkle work surface with 1 Tbsp. powdered sugar. Roll 1 piecrust into a 12½-inch circle, and cut into 3 (6-inch) rounds. Repeat with remaining 3 piecrusts and 3 Tbsp. powdered sugar to make 12 rounds. Fit 6 rounds, sugar sides down, into each mold of a 6-cavity mini pie pan; fold edges under, and crimp. Prick bottom and sides with a fork. Chill remaining 6 rounds. Bake at 425° for 8 minutes or until golden brown. Cool on a wire rack 5 minutes. Remove crusts from pan to wire rack, and cool completely. Cool pan completely. Repeat procedure with remaining 6 piecrust rounds.

2. Prepare Creamy Lemon Filling: Beat cream cheese and sour cream at medium speed with an electric mixer until smooth. Add ½ cup granulated sugar and next 2 ingredients; beat until smooth and fluffy. Spread about 2½ Tbsp. filling into each cooled piecrust; cover with plastic wrap, and chill until ready to serve (up to 24 hours).

3. Prepare Strawberry Topping: Process 1½ cups chopped strawberries in a blender or food processor until smooth, and press through a wire-mesh strainer into a 3-qt. saucepan, using back of a spoon to squeeze out juice; discard pulp. Stir 1 cup granulated sugar into juice in pan. Whisk together cornstarch and ¼ cup water; gradually whisk cornstarch mixture into strawberry mixture. Bring to a boil over medium heat, and cook, whisking constantly, 1 minute. Remove from heat, and whisk in butter. Cool 15 minutes. Gently toss together strawberry mixture and 10 cups hulled strawberries in a large bowl until coated. (Halve some berries; leave others whole.) Cover; chill 3 hours or until cold.

4. Prepare Vanilla Cream: Beat heavy cream and vanilla at medium-high speed until foamy; gradually add powdered sugar, beating until soft peaks form. Spoon about ½ cup Strawberry Topping into each pie; top with Vanilla Cream. Serve immediately.

INDIVIDUAL BERRY PIES

(pictured on page 202)

Use small circle cookie cutters to create simple decorative top crusts that mimic the shape of the berries inside while also giving a peek at the bubbling fruit filling.

makes 10 pies   hands-on 30 min.   total 1 hour, 5 min.

2 (6-oz.) packages fresh raspberries	4 recipes Simple Piecrust, prepared
1 cup chopped fresh strawberries	through Step 1, divided (page 214)
½ cup sugar	2 Tbsp. butter, cubed
2 Tbsp. cornstarch	1 large egg yolk
½ tsp. almond extract	1 Tbsp. sugar

1. Preheat oven to 425°. Gently toss together first 5 ingredients.

2. On a lightly floured surface, roll 2 recipes of Simple Piecrust to ¼-inch thickness. Cut crusts into 10 rounds using a 4-inch round cutter. Fit into 10 lightly greased 3-inch fluted tart pans; press into edges. Spoon berry mixture into pans; dot with butter.

3. On a lightly floured surface, roll remaining 2 recipes of Simple Piecrust to ¼-inch thickness. Cut into 10 (4-inch) rounds. Cut small circles from top of each round using small round cookie cutters. Place rounds over filling in each tart pan; press into fluted edges to seal. Top each tart with circles, leaving cutouts open for steam to escape. Freeze pies on an aluminum foil-lined 15- x 10-inch jelly-roll pan 10 minutes.

4. Meanwhile, whisk together egg yolk and 1 Tbsp. water. Brush tops of pies with egg mixture; sprinkle with 1 Tbsp. sugar.

5. Bake pies on jelly-roll pan at 425° for 24 to 26 minutes or until bubbly and golden brown.

Tip: Feel free to cut any shape you like into the top crusts such as stars, hearts, or circles. Or, keep tops whole, if desired; cut 3 slits in each for steam to escape.

xxxxxxxxxxxxxxxxxxxxxxxxxxxxxxxxxxxxxxx

time-saving tip

These pies can easily be made with store-bought piecrusts as well. Substitute 2 (15-oz.) boxes refrigerated piecrusts for the 4 recipes Simple Piecrust, and follow recipe as directed.

xxxxxxxxxxxxxxxxxxxxxxxxxxxxxxxxxxxxxxx

APPLE SLAB PIE

(pictured on page 203)

Baked in a jelly-roll pan and cut into squares, this rectangular pie feeds a crowd.

makes 12 to 14 servings   hands-on 35 min.   total 3 hours, 5 min.

Crust:
5   cups all-purpose flour
2   Tbsp. granulated sugar
1   Tbsp. ground cinnamon
1   tsp. table salt
2   cups cold butter, cubed
1½ cups ice-cold water

Filling:
2   Tbsp. butter
3   lb. tart apples, peeled and sliced
    (about 6 large)
1   cup dried cranberries

½   cup firmly packed dark brown sugar
½   cup amaretto liqueur (optional)
6   Tbsp. cornstarch
3   Tbsp. fresh lemon juice
1½ tsp. table salt
1   tsp. ground ginger
1   tsp. ground cinnamon
1   tsp. ground allspice

Remaining Ingredients:
2   Tbsp. heavy cream
1   large egg

1. Prepare Crust: Stir together first 4 ingredients in a large bowl. Cut butter into flour mixture with a pastry blender or fork until mixture resembles small peas. Gently stir in ¾ cup ice-cold water until blended. Add remaining ¾ cup ice-cold water, and stir until a dough forms. Shape into a ball, using your hands.

2. Turn dough out onto a floured surface, and knead lightly 10 times or until dough begins to look smooth. Divide in half, and shape into two 7- x 5-inch rectangles. Wrap rectangles in plastic wrap, and chill 1 hour.

3. Prepare Filling: Melt 2 Tbsp. butter in a Dutch oven or large saucepan over medium heat. Add apples; cook, stirring occasionally, 3 minutes. Increase heat to medium-high, and add cranberries and next 8 ingredients. Cook, stirring occasionally, 3 minutes. Remove from heat, and chill 20 minutes.

4. Assemble Pie: Preheat oven to 375°. Line a 15- x 10-inch jelly-roll pan with 2 layers of aluminum foil, allowing 2 to 3 inches to extend over short sides.

5. Roll 1 dough rectangle into a 20- x 15-inch rectangle (about ¼ inch thick) on lightly floured surface. Transfer to prepared pan, allowing dough to extend over edges. Gently press dough into corners of pan. Top with apple mixture. Chill until ready to use.

6. Whisk together cream and egg. Roll remaining dough into a 20- x 15-inch rectangle (about ¼ inch thick) on lightly floured surface. Cut into 1-inch strips. Place strips over apple mixture in a lattice pattern, pressing ends to adhere. Trim excess dough from top and the bottom crusts; crimp edges, if desired. Brush with egg mixture.

7. Bake at 375° for 1 hour to 1 hour and 10 minutes or until golden and bubbly. Cool on a wire rack 10 minutes. Lift pie from pan, using foil sides as handles, and transfer to wire rack. Serve warm or at room temperature.

Note: Dough may be chilled up to 3 days or frozen up to 1 month.

~ bourbon ~

Ask just about any Southerner and he or she will tell you that bourbon whiskey is the best brown liquor on the planet. We love to cook with it, bake with it, or just drink it down. And while all bourbon is whiskey, not all whiskey is bourbon. For one, bourbon must be American made to be legally called bourbon. Two, bourbon has to be at least 51% corn, that's the grain that makes the mash. And three, it has to be aged in a new white oak barrel.

BOURBON PIE WITH TIPSY BERRIES

Similar to a buttermilk pie but spiked with bourbon, this recipe can be made either with regular or chocolate-flavored graham cracker crumbs.

makes 8 servings   hands-on 15 min.   total 3 hours, 25 min., including berries

1⅔ cups finely crushed graham cracker crumbs*
3 Tbsp. sugar
¼ cup butter, melted
2 Tbsp. all-purpose flour
1 cup sugar
3 large eggs, beaten

1 cup buttermilk
½ cup butter, melted
2 Tbsp. bourbon
1 tsp. vanilla extract
⅛ tsp. sea salt
Pinch of freshly grated nutmeg
Tipsy Berries

1. Preheat oven to 350°. Stir together first 3 ingredients; firmly press on bottom and up sides of a 9-inch pie plate. Bake at 350° for 10 to 12 minutes or until fragrant. Cool completely on a wire rack (about 30 minutes). Reduce oven temperature to 325°.

2. Whisk together flour and 1 cup sugar. Whisk in eggs until sugar is dissolved. Whisk in buttermilk and next 5 ingredients until smooth. Pour into crust.

3. Bake at 325° for 45 to 50 minutes or until puffy and golden. Cool completely on a wire rack (about 1 hour). Chill until ready to serve. Serve with Tipsy Berries.

* Chocolate graham crackers may be substituted.

TIPSY BERRIES

This medley of berries is a summery spin on ambrosia. They are elegant, easy to prepare, and add a pop of color to our Bourbon Pie.

1 (16-oz.) container fresh strawberries, sliced
1 cup fresh blueberries
½ cup fresh raspberries

¼ cup shaved fresh coconut
2 Tbsp. bourbon
2 tsp. sugar

Stir together strawberries, blueberries, raspberries, coconut, bourbon, and sugar. Let stand 30 minutes. Serve with a slotted spoon. **Makes about 2½ cups.**

HONEY~BALSAMIC~ BLUEBERRY PIE

A touch of tangy-sweet balsamic vinegar, combined with honey, cinnamon, and a pinch of freshly ground black pepper, magnifies the sweetness of blueberries. We love this buttery crust, but if time is short, substitute a store-bought one and simply crimp the edges.

makes 8 servings   hands-on 35 min.   total 5 hours, 5 min.

Crust:
3   cups all-purpose flour
¾   cup cold butter, sliced
6   Tbsp. cold vegetable shortening, sliced
1   tsp. kosher salt
4   to 6 Tbsp. ice-cold water

Filling:
7   cups fresh blueberries
¼   cup cornstarch

2   Tbsp. balsamic vinegar
½   cup sugar
⅓   cup honey
1   tsp. vanilla extract
¼   tsp. kosher salt
¼   tsp. ground cinnamon
⅛   tsp. finely ground black pepper
Butter
2   Tbsp. butter, cut into ¼-inch cubes
1   large egg

1. Prepare Crust: Process first 4 ingredients in a food processor until mixture resembles coarse meal. With processor running, gradually add 4 Tbsp. ice-cold water, 1 Tbsp. at a time, and process until dough forms a ball and pulls away from sides of bowl, adding up to 2 Tbsp. more water, 1 Tbsp. at a time, if necessary. Divide dough in half, and flatten each half into a disk. Wrap each disk in plastic wrap, and chill 2 hours to 2 days.

2. Prepare Filling: Place 1 cup blueberries in a large bowl; crush blueberries with a wooden spoon. Stir cornstarch and vinegar into crushed berries until cornstarch dissolves. Stir sugar, next 5 ingredients, and remaining 6 cups blueberries into crushed berry mixture.

3. Unwrap 1 dough disk, and place on a lightly floured surface. Sprinkle with flour. Roll dough to ⅛-inch thickness. Fit dough into a greased (with butter) 9-inch deep-dish pie plate. Repeat rolling procedure with remaining dough disk; cut dough into 12 to 14 (½-inch-wide) strips. (You will have dough left over.)

4. Pour blueberry mixture into piecrust, and dot with butter cubes. Arrange piecrust strips in a lattice design over filling. Trim excess dough.

5. Reroll remaining dough, and cut into 6 (9- x ½-inch) strips. Twist together 2 strips at a time. Whisk together egg and 1 Tbsp. water. Brush a small amount of egg mixture around edge of pie. Arrange twisted strips around edge of pie, pressing lightly to adhere. Brush entire pie with remaining egg mixture. Freeze 20 minutes or until dough is firm.

6. Preheat oven to 425°. Bake pie on an aluminum foil-lined baking sheet at 425° for 20 minutes. Reduce oven temperature to 375°, and bake 20 more minutes. Cover pie with aluminum foil to prevent excessive browning, and bake 25 to 30 more minutes (65 to 70 minutes total) or until crust is golden and filling bubbles in center. Remove from baking sheet to a wire rack; cool 1 hour before serving.

Key limes

Hailing from the tropical beaches of the Florida Keys, the smaller, yellow-green, thin-skinned cousin of the Persian lime has its own distinct flavor and a little more tartness. If you're making a true Key lime pie, there's really no substitute, but the bottled juice can be a little easier to find than the whole fresh Key limes.

TEQUILA-KEY LIME MERINGUE PIE

Florida's revered Key limes collide with a south-of-the-border spirit in a luscious Key lime pie that becomes a showstopper with a mountain of meringue.

makes 8 servings   hands-on 30 min.   total 4 hours, 10 min.

1½ cups graham cracker crumbs
6   Tbsp. melted butter
⅓   cup sugar
1   tsp. ground cinnamon
¼   tsp. kosher salt
8   large egg yolks
2   (14-oz.) cans sweetened condensed milk
2   Tbsp. lime zest
¾   cup Key lime juice

1   Tbsp. tequila
3   Tbsp. cold water
1½ Tbsp. cornstarch
⅔   cup boiling water
4   large egg whites
1½ tsp. cream of tartar
1   cup sugar
1½ tsp. vanilla extract
⅛   tsp. kosher salt

1. Preheat oven to 350°. Stir together first 5 ingredients; firmly press mixture on bottom and up sides of a lightly greased 9-inch deep-dish pie plate. Bake at 350° for 15 minutes or until lightly browned. Transfer to a wire rack, and cool completely (about 30 minutes).

2. Whisk together egg yolks and next 4 ingredients in a large bowl; pour mixture into cooled crust. Bake at 350° for 25 minutes or until set. Cool completely on wire rack (about 1 hour).

3. Increase oven temperature to 375°. Whisk 3 Tbsp. cold water into cornstarch in a 1-qt. saucepan; whisk in ⅔ cup boiling water. Cook over medium heat, whisking constantly, 1 minute or until a thick gel forms. Remove from heat; cool completely (about 30 minutes).

4. Beat 4 egg whites and cream of tartar at medium-high speed with a heavy-duty electric stand mixer, using whisk attachment, until foamy. Gradually add 1 cup sugar; beat until stiff peaks form and sugar dissolves (about 2 to 4 minutes). Beat in vanilla and salt. Slowly beat in cornstarch mixture. Beat 3 minutes.

5. Spread meringue over cooled pie, and bake at 375° for 15 minutes or until meringue is golden brown. Transfer to wire rack, and cool completely (about 45 minutes). Serve at room temperature, or cover and chill 8 to 24 hours.

CLASSIC SOUTHERN BUTTERMILK PIE

Bake a sweet memory with this old-time favorite custard pie that's similar to chess pie without the cornmeal. One bite of this creamy pie will take you back in time.

makes 8 servings   hands-on 10 min.   total 3 hours, 47 min.

1½ cups sugar
3   Tbsp. all-purpose flour
3   large eggs
1   cup buttermilk
½   cup butter, melted
1   Tbsp. loosely packed lemon zest

3   Tbsp. fresh lemon juice
1   tsp. vanilla extract
Simple Piecrust
Garnishes: fresh berries, whipped cream,
     fresh mint

1. Preheat oven to 350°. Whisk together first 2 ingredients in a large bowl. Whisk eggs and next 5 ingredients into flour mixture; pour into Simple Piecrust.

2. Bake at 350° for 35 to 45 minutes or until almost set, shielding edges with aluminum foil after 15 minutes. Transfer to a wire rack, and cool 1 hour.

SIMPLE PIECRUST

1¼ cups all-purpose flour
½   cup cold butter, cut into pieces

¼   tsp. table salt
4   or 5 Tbsp. ice water

1. Combine first 3 ingredients in a large bowl with a pastry blender until mixture resembles small peas. Sprinkle ice water, 1 Tbsp. at a time, over surface of mixture in bowl, and stir with a fork until dry ingredients are moistened. Shape into a ball; cover and chill 30 minutes.

2. Preheat oven to 425°. Roll dough into a 13-inch circle on a lightly floured surface. Fit into a 9-inch pie plate; fold edges under, and crimp. Line pastry with aluminum foil; fill with pie weights or dried beans.

3. Bake at 425° for 15 minutes. Remove weights and foil; bake 5 to 10 more minutes or until golden brown. Cool completely on a wire rack. **Makes 1 (9-inch) piecrust.**

216

HOT FUDGE PIE

Made with both melted bittersweet chocolate and cocoa powder, there's no denying the intensity of this rich and decadent pie. Fudgy like a brownie, this pie's custard filling is velvety and smooth thanks to a generous helping of whole eggs and egg yolks.

makes 8 servings   hands-on 5 min.   total 1 hour, 5 min.

1   cup half-and-half
¼   cup butter
8   oz. bittersweet chocolate, chopped
1½   cups sugar
¾   cup unsweetened cocoa
¼   cup all-purpose flour

¼   tsp. table salt
2   large eggs
3   large egg yolks
Simple Piecrust, prepared through
    Step 2 (page 214)

1. Microwave half-and-half, butter, and chopped bittersweet chocolate in a microwave-safe bowl at HIGH 1½ to 2 minutes or until chocolate is melted and smooth, stirring at 30-second intervals. Stir together sugar, cocoa, flour, and salt in a medium bowl. Stir in eggs, egg yolks, and melted chocolate mixture. Use immediately, or pour filling into a 1-qt. jar; let cool. Store filling in refrigerator up to 7 days. (Mixture will thicken as it chills.)

2. Preheat oven to 350°. Prepare Simple Piecrust, fitting crust into a 9-inch deep-dish pie plate. Pour filling into prepared crust; bake at 350° for 45 minutes or until filling puffs, center is set, and top begins to crack around the edges. Cool 10 minutes before serving.

⁓ BAKING SECRETS ⁓
from the Southern Living Test Kitchen

Chocolate can be melted in a heavy pan over low heat on the cooktop or in a microwave-safe container in the microwave. Be sure all utensils are very dry, because even a little water will cause the chocolate to stiffen and become lumpy or seize. Only heat chocolate a little at a time while stirring often; as soon as it's almost all melted and smooth, remove it from heat, and it will continue melting as you stir.

Lemon-Almond Tarts with Fresh Raspberries

Plum Shortbread Tart

Coconut Cream Tarts with
Macadamia Nut Crusts

Strawberry-Orange
Shortcake Tart

LEMON-ALMOND TARTS WITH FRESH RASPBERRIES

(pictured on page 218)

While any small fresh berry would happily adorn these little tarts, we found that raspberries perfectly complement the rich lemon and almond filling, and they are readily available almost any time of the year.

makes 6 (4-inch) tarts   hands-on 30 min.   total 3 hours

Vanilla Wafer Crusts:
75 vanilla wafers
¼   cup powdered sugar
½   cup butter, melted

Lemon-Almond Filling:
1   (7-oz.) package almond paste
2   large eggs

¼   cup granulated sugar
2   Tbsp. melted butter
⅔   cup lemon curd
2   (6-oz.) packages fresh raspberries
Garnish: chopped sliced almonds

1. Prepare Vanilla Wafer Crusts: Preheat oven to 350°. Pulse vanilla wafers in a food processor 8 to 10 times or until finely crushed. Stir together crushed wafers, powdered sugar, and butter in a medium bowl. Press crumb mixture on bottom and up sides of 6 lightly greased 4-inch tart pans with removable bottoms. Place on a baking sheet.

2. Bake at 350° for 10 to 12 minutes or until lightly browned. Transfer to a wire rack. Let cool completely (about 30 minutes). Reduce oven temperature to 325°.

3. Prepare Lemon-Almond Filling: Beat almond paste and next 3 ingredients at medium speed with an electric mixer until well blended. Pour mixture into crusts.

4. Bake at 325° for 18 to 20 minutes or until set and just beginning to brown around edges. Let cool on a wire rack 30 minutes. Spread 1½ Tbsp. lemon curd onto each tart. Cover and chill 1 to 24 hours. Remove tarts from pans, and top with raspberries just before serving.

Note: Find almond paste in the baking aisle, either in a tube-shaped plastic wrapper (which we call for in this recipe) or a can. If you find it only in a can, use ¾ cup. We tested with Odense Pure Almond Paste.

BAKING SECRETS
from the Southern Living Test Kitchen

Almond paste is a firm but pliable paste made mostly of ground blanched almonds and sugar. While it's similar to marzipan, almond paste is a little coarser and not as sweet.

COCONUT CREAM TARTS WITH MACADAMIA NUT CRUSTS

(pictured on page 219)

The classic drugstore counter favorite gets a new twist with a crisp,
nutty crust that adds crunchy contrast to the beloved custard filling.

makes 1 dozen (3- to 4-inch) tarts   hands-on 1 hour   total 5 hours, 25 min.

⅓ cup all-purpose flour
¾ cup sugar
4 large eggs
2 cups milk
1 Tbsp. vanilla extract
1½ cups sweetened flaked coconut, divided

2½ cups all-purpose flour
¾ cup cold butter, cut up
1½ cups macadamia nuts, chopped
1 cup whipping cream
3 Tbsp. sugar

1. Stir together ⅓ cup flour and ¾ cup sugar; whisk in eggs.

2. Cook milk in a heavy saucepan over medium heat until hot. Gradually whisk about one-fourth of hot milk into egg mixture; add to remaining hot milk, whisking constantly. Cook over medium-high heat, whisking constantly, 5 to 6 minutes or until thickened. Remove from heat; stir in vanilla and 1 cup coconut. Cover and chill 3 hours.

3. Preheat oven to 350°. Bake remaining ½ cup coconut in a shallow pan at 350°, stirring occasionally, 5 to 6 minutes or until toasted; set aside.

4. Pulse 2½ cups flour and butter in a food processor until crumbly. Add 2 Tbsp. water, and pulse 30 seconds or until dough forms a ball. Turn out onto a lightly floured surface; knead in nuts. Divide dough into 12 equal portions; press each portion into a (3- to 4-inch) tart pan. Prick bottoms with a fork, and place on a 15- x 10-inch jelly-roll pan. Cover and freeze 30 minutes.

5. Preheat oven to 375°. Bake on jelly-roll pan for 15 to 20 minutes or until golden. Cool in tart pans 5 minutes; remove from pans, and cool completely on a wire rack (about 30 minutes).

6. Spoon coconut custard mixture into tart shells. Beat whipping cream and 3 Tbsp. sugar at high speed with an electric mixer until soft peaks form; dollop or pipe onto tarts. Sprinkle with toasted coconut; serve immediately, or chill up to 2 hours.

PLUM SHORTBREAD TART

(pictured on page 218)

*The natural pairing of stone fruits and almonds in this tart gets
livened up with just a splash of amaretto in the custard filling.*

makes 8 servings   hands-on 30 min.   total 2 hours, 24 min.

Crust:
- ¾ cup all-purpose flour
- ¼ cup toasted slivered almonds
- Pinch of sea salt
- ⅓ cup powdered sugar
- ¼ cup butter, softened
- 1 large egg yolk

Filling:
- 6 large egg yolks
- ½ cup sugar
- 6 Tbsp. all-purpose flour
- Pinch of sea salt
- 2 cups milk
- 1 Tbsp. loosely packed lemon zest
- 2 Tbsp. butter
- 2 Tbsp. amaretto liqueur
- 4 plums, thinly sliced
- 1 Tbsp. warm apricot preserves
- Garnish: fresh mint leaves

1. Prepare Crust: Preheat oven to 350°. Pulse flour, almonds, and sea salt in a food processor 3 times or until combined.

2. Beat powdered sugar and softened butter at medium speed with an electric mixer 5 minutes or until pale and fluffy. Gradually add flour mixture and egg yolk, beating at low speed until a dough forms. Press dough into a lightly greased 13- x 4-inch tart pan with removable bottom. Chill 10 minutes.

3. Bake at 350° for 14 minutes or until golden. Cool completely.

4. Prepare Filling: Whisk egg yolks until thick and pale. Whisk together sugar, flour, and sea salt. Combine milk and lemon zest in a saucepan; cook over medium heat, stirring constantly, 5 minutes or just until it begins to steam. Add sugar mixture, whisking constantly just until bubbles appear. Gradually stir one-fourth of hot milk mixture into yolks; add to remaining hot milk mixture, stirring constantly. Bring mixture to a low boil over medium heat; remove from heat.

5. Stir in butter and amaretto liqueur. Transfer to a bowl; place plastic wrap directly onto warm custard (to prevent a film from forming). Cool 1 hour. Mixture will thicken as it cools. Spread into crust; top with thinly sliced plums. Brush with warm apricot preserves.

STRAWBERRY~ORANGE SHORTCAKE TART

(pictured on page 219)

Baking the shortcake in a tart pan produces a sweet-and-sturdy
biscuit-like base for the fresh, seasonal berries and whipped cream.
If the berries are very ripe, you may want to decrease the amount of sugar.

makes 8 servings   hands-on 20 min.   total 1 hour, 25 min.

1¾	cups all-purpose flour	1	Tbsp. orange marmalade
¼	cup plain yellow cornmeal	1	(16-oz.) container fresh strawberries, cut in half
2	Tbsp. sugar		
¾	tsp. baking powder	½	cup orange marmalade
½	tsp. table salt	2	cups heavy cream
6	Tbsp. cold butter, cut into pieces	2	Tbsp. sugar
1	large egg, lightly beaten		Garnishes: fresh mint sprigs, sweetened whipped cream
⅔	cup buttermilk		

1. Preheat oven to 425°. Place first 6 ingredients (in order of ingredient list) in a food processor. Process 20 seconds or until mixture resembles coarse sand. Transfer to a large bowl.

2. Whisk together egg and buttermilk; add to flour mixture, stirring just until dry ingredients are moistened and a dough forms. Turn dough out onto a lightly floured surface, and knead 3 or 4 times. Press dough on bottom and up sides of a lightly greased 9-inch tart pan.

3. Bake at 425° for 20 to 22 minutes or until golden and firm to touch. Microwave 1 Tbsp. marmalade at HIGH 10 seconds; brush over crust. Cool 45 minutes.

4. Stir together strawberries and ½ cup marmalade. Beat heavy cream with 2 Tbsp. sugar at medium speed with an electric mixer until soft peaks form. Spoon onto cornmeal crust; top with strawberry mixture.

STRAWBERRY-RHUBARB TARTLETS

A sure sign of spring, rhubarb has a fleeting season. The sweet strawberries in these flaky little treats add welcome sweetness to an otherwise mouth-puckering perennial vegetable.

makes 2 dozen tartlets   hands-on 40 min.   total 3 hours, 15 min.

Tartlet Dough
3   Tbsp. butter
½   cup sliced fresh or frozen rhubarb
1   cup sliced fresh strawberries
⅔   cup granulated sugar
1   Tbsp. all-purpose flour

3   Tbsp. fresh lemon juice, divided
Parchment paper
1   large egg
2½ Tbsp. milk, divided
1½ cups powdered sugar

1. Prepare Tartlet Dough.

2. Melt butter in a 1-qt. saucepan over medium heat. Add rhubarb, and sauté 3 minutes. Stir in strawberries and ⅔ cup granulated sugar; cook, stirring constantly and crushing fruit with spoon, 5 minutes.

3. Stir together 1 Tbsp. flour and 2 Tbsp. lemon juice until smooth. Stir juice mixture into rhubarb mixture; bring to a boil. Cook, stirring often, 2 minutes or until thickened. Remove from heat, and transfer mixture to a small bowl. Cover and chill 30 minutes.

4. Preheat oven to 350°. Unwrap Tartlet Dough; roll each disk to ⅛-inch thickness on a floured surface. Cut dough into 48 rectangles, using a 2½- x 3-inch cutter and rerolling scraps. Place half of dough rectangles 2 inches apart on parchment paper-lined baking sheets. Top each rectangle with about 1 Tbsp. strawberry mixture. Dampen edges of dough with water, and top with remaining dough rectangles, pressing edges to seal.

5. Stir together egg and 2 Tbsp. milk, and brush over tops of tarts. Cut a small "X" in top of each tartlet for steam to escape.

6. Bake tartlets at 350° for 30 to 35 minutes or until golden. Transfer tartlets to a wire rack; cool 15 minutes. Whisk together powdered sugar and remaining 1 Tbsp. lemon juice and 1½ tsp. milk; drizzle over tartlets.

TARTLET DOUGH

2½ cups all-purpose flour
¼   cup sugar
¼   tsp. table salt
¼   tsp. baking powder

1   cup cold butter, cut into small pieces
2   large egg yolks
½   cup ice-cold water

Pulse first 4 ingredients in a food processor until blended. Add cold butter, and pulse 5 or 6 times or just until mixture resembles coarse meal. Stir together egg yolks and ice-cold water. With processor running, pour yolk mixture through food chute, and process just until mixture forms a ball and pulls away from sides of bowl. Divide dough in half, and form into disks. Wrap disks in plastic wrap; chill 1 hour. **Makes enough for 2 dozen tartlets.**

ELEGANT CITRUS TART

Topping our tart are Florida-grown Ruby Red grapefruit and navel oranges and the brightest red grapefruit you can buy—the Rio Star from Texas.

makes 8 servings   hands-on 20 min.   total 10 hours, 5 min., including curd

⅓ cup sweetened flaked coconut
2 cups all-purpose flour
⅔ cup powdered sugar
¾ cup cold butter, cut into pieces

¼ tsp. coconut extract
Buttery Orange Curd
9 assorted citrus fruits, peeled and
    sectioned

1. Preheat oven to 350°. Bake coconut in a single layer in a shallow pan 4 to 5 minutes or until toasted and fragrant, stirring halfway through; cool completely (about 15 minutes).

2. Pulse coconut, flour, and powdered sugar in a food processor 3 or 4 times or until combined. Add butter and coconut extract, and pulse 5 or 6 times or until crumbly. With processor running, gradually add 3 Tbsp. water, and process until dough forms a ball and leaves sides of bowl.

3. Roll dough into a 12½- x 8-inch rectangle (about ¼ inch thick) on a lightly floured surface; press on bottom and up sides of a 12- x 9-inch tart pan with removable bottom. Trim excess dough, and discard.

4. Bake at 350° for 30 minutes. Cool completely on a wire rack (about 40 minutes).

5. Spread Buttery Orange Curd over crust. Top with citrus sections.

Note: To make a round tart, roll dough into a 10-inch circle (about ¼ inch thick) on a lightly floured surface; press on bottom and up sides of a 9-inch round tart pan with removable bottom. Trim excess dough, and discard. Bake as directed.

BUTTERY ORANGE CURD

⅔ cup sugar
2½ Tbsp. cornstarch
1⅓ cups orange juice
1 large egg, lightly beaten

3 Tbsp. butter
2 tsp. loosely packed orange zest
Pinch of table salt

1. Combine sugar and cornstarch in a 3-qt. saucepan; gradually whisk in orange juice. Whisk in egg. Bring to a boil; boil, whisking constantly, 3 to 4 minutes.

2. Remove from heat; whisk in butter, zest, and salt. Place heavy-duty plastic wrap directly on warm curd (to prevent a film from forming), and chill 8 hours. Store leftovers in refrigerator up to 3 days. **Makes about 2 cups.**

Note: We tested with Simply Orange 100% Pure Squeezed Orange Juice.

227

SALTED CARAMEL~ CHOCOLATE PECAN TART

A cross between a chocolate tart and pecan pie, this is all the more stunning if you arrange autumn's new-crop Southern pecan halves from the center in a spiral pattern.

makes 8 servings   hands-on 25 min.   total 1 hour, 20 min.

Tart Shell:
1   recipe Simple Piecrust, prepared through Step 2 (page 214)

Chocolate Filling:
1½ cups sugar
¾   cup butter, melted
⅓   cup all-purpose flour
⅓   cup 100% cacao unsweetened cocoa
1   Tbsp. light corn syrup
1   tsp. vanilla extract
3   large eggs
1   cup toasted chopped pecans

Salted Caramel Topping:
¾   cup sugar
1   Tbsp. fresh lemon juice
⅓   cup heavy cream
4   Tbsp. butter
¼   tsp. table salt
2   cups toasted pecan halves
½   tsp. sea salt

1. Prepare Tart Shell: Preheat oven to 350°. Fit piecrust into a 10-inch tart pan with removable bottom.

2. Prepare Chocolate Filling: Stir together first 6 ingredients in a large bowl. Add eggs, stirring until well blended. Fold in chopped pecans. Pour mixture into tart shell.

3. Bake at 350° for 35 minutes. (Filling will be loose but will set as it cools.) Remove from oven to a wire rack.

4. Prepare Salted Caramel Topping: Bring ¾ cup sugar, 1 Tbsp. lemon juice, and ¼ cup water to a boil in a medium saucepan over high heat. (Do not stir.) Boil, swirling occasionally after sugar begins to change color, 8 minutes or until dark amber. (Do not walk away from the pan, as the sugar could burn quickly once it begins to change color.) Remove from heat; add cream and 4 Tbsp. butter. Stir constantly until bubbling stops and butter is incorporated (about 1 minute). Stir in table salt.

5. Arrange pecan halves on tart. Top with warm caramel. Cool 15 minutes; sprinkle with sea salt.

Note: We tested with Hershey's 100% Cacao Special Dark Cocoa and Maldon Sea Salt Flakes.

Patchwork
Cobbler

Cranberry-Pear
Crisp

Apple-Cherry
Cobbler with
Pinwheel Biscuits

Peach-Berry
Crumble

PATCHWORK COBBLER

(pictured on page 230)

*Topped with squares of sugar-crusted pastry, this cobbler shows
off summer fruits in a rich, just-sweet-enough filling.*

makes 10 to 12 servings   hands-on 30 min.   total 3 hours, 10 min.

Crust:

2   cups all-purpose flour
3   Tbsp. granulated sugar
¼   tsp. table salt
1   cup cold butter, cut into pieces
1   large egg yolk
3   Tbsp. ice-cold milk

Filling:

8   cups peeled and sliced firm,
     ripe peaches (about 7 large or 3 lb.)

6   cups sliced red plums (about 9 medium
     or 2 lb.)
2   cups fresh blueberries
2   tsp. vanilla extract
1¾ cups granulated sugar
½   cup all-purpose flour
¼   cup butter, melted
1   large egg
Sanding sugar or sparkling sugar

1. Prepare Crust: Stir together first 3 ingredients in a large bowl. Cut 1 cup butter into flour mixture with a pastry blender until mixture resembles coarse meal. Whisk together egg yolk and milk; stir into flour mixture just until dough starts to form a ball. Shape dough into a flat disk using lightly floured hands. Wrap disk in plastic wrap, and chill 1 to 24 hours.

2. Prepare Filling: Preheat oven to 425°. Place peaches and next 3 ingredients in a large bowl. Stir together 1¾ cups sugar and ½ cup flour; sprinkle over peach mixture, and gently stir. Spoon into a lightly greased 13- x 9-inch or shallow 3-qt. baking dish. Drizzle with melted butter.

3. Place dough disk on a lightly floured surface; sprinkle with flour. Place a piece of plastic wrap over dough disk. (This makes the dough easier to roll.) Roll dough to ⅛-inch to ¼-inch thickness; cut into 2-inch squares. Arrange squares in a patchwork pattern over peach mixture, leaving openings for steam to escape.

4. Whisk together egg and 2 Tbsp. water; brush dough with egg mixture. Sprinkle with sanding sugar or sparkling sugar.

5. Bake on lowest oven rack at 425° for 40 to 55 minutes or until crust is deep golden and peach mixture is bubbly, shielding edges with foil during last 5 to 10 minutes to prevent excessive browning. Transfer to a wire rack; cool 1 hour.

CRANBERRY~PEAR CRISP

(pictured on page 230)

It doesn't get any easier than a crisp. Save yourself the heartache at the holidays and make this cranberry-studded spiced pear dessert with a crumbly oat topping; your guests will be content, and you'll still have your wits about you.

makes 8 servings   hands-on 20 min.   total 40 min.

⅔   cup granulated sugar
2   tsp. ground cinnamon
1½ tsp. ground ginger
1½ cups fresh orange juice
1   (12-oz.) package fresh cranberries
6   pears, thinly sliced

2   tsp. loosely packed orange zest
1½ cups uncooked regular oats
⅔   cup all-purpose flour
⅔   cup firmly packed brown sugar
½   cup butter

1. Preheat oven to 375°. Combine first 7 ingredients in a large saucepan; bring to a boil. Reduce heat, and simmer, stirring occasionally, 10 minutes or until cranberry skins begin to split and mixture begins to thicken. Spoon evenly into a lightly greased 13- x 9-inch baking dish.

2. Combine oats, flour, and brown sugar in a large bowl; cut in butter with a pastry blender until crumbly. Sprinkle over fruit mixture.

3. Bake at 375° for 20 to 25 minutes or until lightly browned. Serve warm.

BAKING SECRETS
from the Southern Living Test Kitchen

If your pears are a little underripe, speed the ripening process along by wrapping pears separately in newspaper and putting them in a cardboard box or paper bag. Let them stand at room temperature until they yield to gentle pressure at the stem end.

APPLE-CHERRY COBBLER WITH PINWHEEL BISCUITS

(*pictured on page 231*)

Try our Southern twist on traditional apple cobbler. Here, buttery biscuit dough is rolled with almonds and brown sugar and bakes into a pretty pinwheel crust.

makes 8 to 10 servings   hands-on 1 hour   total 1 hour, 15 min.

Apple-Cherry Filling:
- 8 large Braeburn apples, peeled and cut into ½-inch-thick wedges (about 4½ lb.)
- 2 cups granulated sugar
- ¼ cup all-purpose flour
- ¼ cup butter
- 1 (12-oz.) package frozen cherries, thawed and well drained
- 1 tsp. loosely packed lemon zest
- ⅓ cup fresh lemon juice
- 1 tsp. ground cinnamon

Pinwheel Biscuits:
- 2¼ cups all-purpose flour
- ¼ cup granulated sugar
- 2¼ tsp. baking powder
- ¾ tsp. table salt
- ¾ cup cold butter, cut into pieces
- ⅔ cup milk
- ⅔ cup firmly packed light brown sugar
- 2 Tbsp. butter, melted
- ¼ cup finely chopped roasted unsalted almonds

Sweetened whipped cream (optional)

1. Prepare Apple-Cherry Filling: Preheat oven to 425°. Toss together first 3 ingredients. Melt ¼ cup butter in a large skillet over medium-high heat; add apple mixture. Cook, stirring often, 20 to 25 minutes or until apples are tender and syrup thickens. Remove from heat; stir in cherries and next 3 ingredients. Spoon apple mixture into a lightly greased 3-qt. baking dish. Bake apple mixture at 425° for 12 minutes, placing a baking sheet on oven rack directly below baking dish to catch any drips.

2. Prepare Pinwheel Biscuits: Stir together 2¼ cups flour and next 3 ingredients in a large bowl. Cut cold butter pieces into flour mixture with a pastry blender or fork until crumbly; stir in milk. Turn dough out onto a lightly floured surface; knead 4 or 5 times. Roll dough into a 12-inch square. Combine brown sugar and 2 Tbsp. melted butter; sprinkle over dough, patting gently. Sprinkle with almonds. Roll up, jelly-roll fashion; pinch seams and ends to seal. Cut roll into 12 (1-inch) slices. Place slices in a single layer on top of apple mixture.

3. Bake at 425° for 15 to 17 minutes or until biscuits are golden. Serve with whipped cream, if desired.

PEACH~BERRY CRUMBLE

(pictured on page 231)

We love this recipe because it's easy enough for busy weeknight cooking; pop the crumble in the oven when you serve dinner and it'll be ready in about 40 minutes. Blueberries or raspberries may be substituted for the blackberries.

makes 6 to 8 servings   hands-on 20 min.   total 1 hour, 10 min.

3   cups fresh peach slices
    (about 3 medium)
2   cups fresh blackberries
1   large egg
1   large egg yolk
1   cup sugar

¾   cup all-purpose flour
½   cup uncooked regular oats
¼   tsp. kosher salt
½   cup butter, melted
Vanilla ice cream

1. Preheat oven to 375°. Place first 2 ingredients in an 11- x 7-inch (or 2-qt.) baking dish.

2. Stir together egg, egg yolk, and next 4 ingredients with a fork until mixture resembles coarse meal. Sprinkle over fruit; drizzle melted butter over topping.

3. Bake at 375° for 40 to 45 minutes or until lightly browned and bubbly. Let stand 10 minutes; serve warm with ice cream.

XXXXXXXXXXXXXXXXXXXXXXXXXXXXXXXXXX

sweet idea

For an extra-special presentation, divide fruit filling and crumble topping among small ramekins, giving each of your guests a treat they don't have to share! The smaller dishes might not take as long to bake, so watch them closely.

XXXXXXXXXXXXXXXXXXXXXXXXXXXXXXXXXX

MINI BERRY COBBLERS

Use a mixture of blueberries, raspberries, blackberries, and strawberries in these charming, individual, summertime desserts.

makes 12 servings   hands-on 25 min.   total 1 hour

18 oz. mixed fresh berries (4 cups)	3 Tbsp. minced crystallized ginger
¼ cup sugar	2 tsp. baking powder
2 Tbsp. butter, melted	½ tsp. table salt
1 Tbsp. cornstarch	⅔ cup cold butter, cubed
1½ cups all-purpose flour	½ cup buttermilk
⅓ cup sugar	Garnish: fresh mint sprigs

1. Preheat oven to 400°. Toss together first 4 ingredients in a medium bowl.

2. Whisk together flour and next 4 ingredients in a large bowl. Cut cold butter into flour mixture with a pastry blender or fork until crumbly. Add buttermilk, stirring just until dry ingredients are moistened. Turn dough out onto a lightly floured surface, and knead 3 or 4 times. Pat into a 6- x 4-inch (1-inch-thick) rectangle. Cut into 6 squares; cut squares diagonally into 12 triangles.

3. Arrange 12 (3½-inch) lightly greased miniature cast-iron skillets on an aluminum foil-lined baking sheet. Divide berry mixture among skillets. Place 1 dough triangle over berry mixture in each skillet.

4. Bake at 400° for 20 to 24 minutes or until fruit bubbles and crust is golden brown. Cool 15 minutes before serving. Serve warm or at room temperature.

BAKING SECRETS
from the Southern Living Test Kitchen

Don't wash berries until you're ready to use them, and wash them before removing the stem. Added moisture will hasten the growth of mold. Washing blueberries before freezing toughens their skins.

BLACKBERRY~PEACH COBBLER WITH PRALINE STREUSEL

While praline generally refers to a caramel-flavored candy,
this streusel is made with the same main ingredients: brown sugar, butter,
and pecans. It's a sweet and crunchy contrast to the baked fresh fruit.

makes 8 servings   hands-on 35 min.   total 1 hour, 10 min.

Streusel:
¾ cup firmly packed light brown sugar
½ cup butter, melted
⅛ tsp. table salt
1½ cups all-purpose flour
1 cup coarsely chopped pecans

Filling:
4 cups peeled and sliced fresh peaches
   (about 4 large)
½ cup granulated sugar
3 Tbsp. all-purpose flour
¼ tsp. ground nutmeg
2 cups fresh blackberries

1. Prepare Streusel: Stir together first 3 ingredients in a large bowl; add flour and pecans, and stir until blended. Let stand 20 minutes or until mixture is firm enough to crumble into small pieces.

2. Prepare Filling: Preheat oven to 375°. Stir together peaches and next 3 ingredients in a large saucepan; bring to a boil over medium-high heat. Reduce heat to medium, and boil, stirring occasionally, 6 to 7 minutes or until juices have thickened. Remove from heat, and stir in blackberries. Spoon mixture into a lightly greased 9-inch square baking dish. Crumble streusel over hot peach mixture.

3. Bake at 375° for 30 to 35 minutes or until bubbly and golden brown.

xxxxxxxxxxxxxxxxxxxxxxxxxxxxxxxxxxxxxxx

time-saving tip
You can use frozen fruit in the recipe in a pinch. Frozen
peaches are already sliced, saving you some time, but you
might need to bake the cobbler 5 to 10 minutes longer.

xxxxxxxxxxxxxxxxxxxxxxxxxxxxxxxxxxxxxxx

cookies, bars
& wafers

COOKIES

*Baking up a batch of cookies just got a little easier
with our simple step-by-step cookie guides.*

Whether soft and chewy or crispy and crunchy, cookies impart a sense of nostalgia that evokes a childlike glee in anyone who takes a bite. Easy enough to whip up on a weeknight, cookies can still cause a bit of heartache if they don't turn out just right. Follow these photo tutorials for making a humble drop cookie, a perfect cut-out cookie, or a gorgeous linzer cookie.

......drop cookies......

Step 1: Line baking sheets with parchment paper or a silicone baking sheet liner.

Step 2: Chill dough for 10 to 15 minutes before scooping onto prepared cookie sheet.

Step 3: Use a 1½-inch cookie scoop to portion cookie dough. Place balls 2 inches apart on baking sheet, or about 12 cookies per standard cookie sheet.

Step 4: Place flour in a small bowl and dip the bottom of a clean, flat-bottomed glass or measuring cup in flour; shake off excess.

Step 5: Gently press floured glass onto cookie balls, flattening them to ½-inch thickness.

Step 6: Bake cookies until edges are lightly browned. Let cool 5 minutes on cookie sheet.

Step 7: Using a metal spatula, transfer cookies to wire rack and let cool completely, about 30 minutes.

.......cut-out cookies.......

Step 1: Divide cookie dough into portions (about 1 cup each).

Step 2: Form each portion into a small disk, about ½ to 1 inch thick.

Step 3: Wrap dough in plastic wrap, and chill at least 1 hour and up to 24 hours.

Step 4: Remove disks of dough from refrigerator 1 at a time while rolling and cutting out cookies.

Step 5: Cold dough can be hard to roll out, so use your rolling pin to firmly press dough to flatten.

Step 6: Roll out dough to ¼-inch thickness, sprinkling additional flour as needed.

Step 7: Cut out desired shapes from dough, and transfer to a parchment paper-lined baking sheet.

Step 8: Bake cookies until edges are lightly browned. Let cool on the pan for 5 minutes, then transfer to a wire rack, and cool completely.

.......linzer cookies.......

Step 1: Roll out dough to ¼-inch thickness; cut into 2-inch fluted rectangles. Cut a 1-inch fluted rectangle out of half of cookies; place on a parchment paper-lined baking sheet.

Step 2: Bake as directed; cool completely. Spread a thin layer of preserves onto whole cookies.

Step 3: Dust cutout cookies with powdered sugar. Place 1 cutout cookie onto each whole cookie.

Step 4: We used raspberry preserves, but any flavor will do. Store cookies in an airtight container at room temperature.

APRICOT~ALMOND THUMBPRINTS

Apricot preserves add dazzle and a delicious jewel-like imprint to these cookies.

makes about 6 dozen cookies   hands-on 30 min.   total 2 hours

2   **cups butter, softened**
⅔   **cup granulated sugar**
⅔   **cup firmly packed light brown sugar**
1   **tsp. almond extract**
¼   **tsp. kosher salt**

4⅔   **cups all-purpose flour**
1½   **cups chopped sliced almonds**
    Parchment paper
¾   **cup apricot preserves**

1. Beat first 5 ingredients at medium speed with an electric mixer 3 to 5 minutes or until creamy. Add flour; beat just until blended.

2. Shape dough into 1-inch balls (about 1 Tbsp. per ball), and roll in almonds. Place 2 inches apart on 2 parchment paper-lined baking sheets. Press thumb or end of a wooden spoon into each ball, forming an indentation. Chill 20 minutes.

3. Preheat oven to 350°. Bake at 350° for 15 minutes or until bottoms are light golden brown. Cool on baking sheets 10 minutes; transfer to wire racks, and cool 10 minutes. Spoon ½ tsp. apricot preserves into each indentation.

~ BAKING SECRETS ~
from the Southern Living Test Kitchen

You might think that by skipping the chill time for cookie dough you could save a little time and get on with baking cookies with no problems. However, the chilling is important to set the shape of the round cookies with the indentation; without it, cookies will spread during baking with no place to put the preserves.

CHOCOLATE CHIP~ OATMEAL COOKIES

Chunky ground oats and chopped pecans give these double-chocolate-studded cookies a great chewy texture and star status.

makes about 4½ dozen cookies   hands-on 25 min.   total 35 min.

2¼ cups uncooked regular oats
2 cups all-purpose flour
1 tsp. baking powder
1 tsp. baking soda
½ tsp. table salt
1 cup unsalted butter, softened
1 cup granulated sugar
1 cup firmly packed light brown sugar

2 large eggs
1 tsp. vanilla extract
1 (12-oz.) package semisweet chocolate morsels
1 (4.4-oz.) milk chocolate candy bar, grated
1½ cups chopped pecans
Parchment paper

1. Preheat oven to 375°. Pulse oats in food processor until finely ground. Whisk together flour, next 3 ingredients, and ground oats in a large bowl.

2. Beat butter and next 2 ingredients at medium speed with an electric mixer until fluffy. Add eggs, 1 at a time, beating just until blended after each addition. Stir in vanilla.

3. Gradually add flour mixture to butter mixture, beating at low speed until blended. Stir in chocolate morsels and next 2 ingredients.

4. Drop dough by level spoonfuls 2 inches apart onto 2 parchment paper-lined jelly-roll pans, using a 1½-inch cookie scoop. Flatten each into a 2-inch circle.

5. Bake at 375° for 8 to 10 minutes or until browned. Cool on pans 2 to 3 minutes; transfer to wire racks.

XXXXXXXXXXXXXXXXXXXXXXXXXXXXXXXXXX

time-saving tip

For freshly baked cookies in a snap, prepare recipe
through Step 4, and freeze cookie dough rounds in
a zip-top plastic freezer bag. When ready to bake,
bake cookies a minute or two longer, or until browned.

XXXXXXXXXXXXXXXXXXXXXXXXXXXXXXXXXX

CRANBERRY-ALMOND COOKIES

Tart fresh cranberries and toasted almonds make a delicious coupling in these irresistible holiday favorites.

makes 3½ dozen cookies   hands-on 25 min.   total 34 min.

1 cup butter, softened
¾ cup granulated sugar
¾ cup firmly packed light brown sugar
½ tsp. almond extract
2 large eggs

2¼ cups all-purpose flour
1 tsp. baking powder
1 tsp. table salt
2 cups chopped fresh cranberries
1 cup slivered almonds, toasted

1. Preheat oven to 375°. Beat butter at medium speed with an electric mixer until creamy; gradually add sugars, beating well. Add almond extract and eggs, beating until blended.

2. Combine flour, baking powder, and salt; gradually add to butter mixture, beating at low speed until blended after each addition. Stir in cranberries and almonds. Drop by rounded tablespoonfuls onto ungreased baking sheets.

3. Bake at 375° for 9 to 11 minutes. Remove to wire racks to cool.

BAKING SECRETS
from the Southern Living Test Kitchen

Allow baking sheets to cool before reusing between baking batches of cookies; wipe the surface with a paper towel or scrape off crumbs with a metal turner.

Mississippi Mud
Cookies

Flourless Peanut Butter-
Chocolate Chip Cookies

Marble
Snickerdoodles

White Chocolate Chip-
Oatmeal Cookies

MISSISSIPPI MUD COOKIES

(pictured on page 250)

Inspired by the pie named for its resemblance to the boggy banks of the Mississippi River, these cookies have the same rich chocolaty, ooey-gooey consistency that made the original recipe famous.

makes about 3 dozen cookies   hands-on 20 min.   total 30 min.

1 cup semisweet chocolate morsels	1 tsp. baking powder
½ cup butter, softened	½ tsp. table salt
1 cup sugar	1 cup chopped pecans
2 large eggs	½ cup milk chocolate morsels
1 tsp. vanilla extract	Parchment paper
1½ cups all-purpose flour	1 cup plus 2 Tbsp. miniature marshmallows

1. Preheat oven to 350°. Microwave semisweet chocolate morsels in a small microwave-safe bowl at HIGH 1 to 1½ minutes or until melted and smooth, stirring at 30-second intervals.

2. Beat butter and sugar at medium speed with an electric mixer until creamy; add eggs, 1 at a time, beating until blended after each addition. Beat in vanilla and melted chocolate.

3. Combine flour, baking powder, and salt; gradually add to chocolate mixture, beating until well blended. Stir in chopped pecans and ½ cup milk chocolate morsels.

4. Drop dough by heaping tablespoonfuls onto parchment paper-lined baking sheets. Press 3 marshmallows into each portion of dough.

5. Bake at 350° for 10 to 12 minutes or until set. Remove to wire racks.

xxxxxxxxxxxxxxxxxxxxxxxxxxxxxxxxxxxx

sweet idea

The bold black and white of these cookies lends them
a spooky look perfect for Halloween. Stack them up and
wrap in wide orange ribbon for the perfect party favor.

xxxxxxxxxxxxxxxxxxxxxxxxxxxxxxxxxxxx

FLOURLESS PEANUT BUTTER~CHOCOLATE CHIP COOKIES

(pictured on page 250)

*These flourless cookies are a dream if you're going gluten-free,
especially with the classic combination of peanut butter and chocolate.*

makes 2 dozen cookies   hands-on 10 min.   total 42 min.

1   cup creamy peanut butter
¾   cup sugar
1   large egg
½   tsp. baking soda
¼   tsp. table salt
1   cup semisweet chocolate morsels
Parchment paper

1. Preheat oven to 350°. Stir together peanut butter and next 4 ingredients in a medium bowl until well blended. Stir in chocolate morsels.

2. Drop dough by rounded tablespoonfuls 2 inches apart onto parchment paper-lined baking sheets.

3. Bake at 350° for 12 to 14 minutes or until puffed and lightly browned. Cool on baking sheets on a wire rack 5 minutes. Transfer to wire rack, and let cool 15 minutes.

BAKING SECRETS
from the Southern Living Test Kitchen

When portioning dough onto the baking sheet, use a tablespoon-sized spoon or scoop, not a measuring spoon. Grab a second spoon to easily push the dough onto the baking sheet.

WHITE CHOCOLATE CHIP~ OATMEAL COOKIES

(pictured on page 251)

Oats go from favorite breakfast fare to dessert in this indulgent twist on traditional chocolate chip cookies. Crunchy pecans balance the sweetness of the white chocolate chips.

makes about 5 dozen cookies   hands-on 25 min.   total 1 hour

1   cup butter, softened
1   cup firmly packed light brown sugar
1   cup granulated sugar
2   large eggs
2   tsp. vanilla extract
3   cups all-purpose flour
1   tsp. baking soda

1   tsp. baking powder
1   tsp. table salt
1½ cups uncooked regular oats
2   cups (12 oz.) white chocolate morsels
1   cup coarsely chopped pecans
Shortening

1. Preheat oven to 350°. Beat butter at medium speed with an electric mixer until creamy; gradually add sugars, beating well. Add eggs, 1 at a time, beating just until blended after each addition. Stir in vanilla.

2. Combine flour and next 3 ingredients; gradually add to butter mixture, beating until blended. Stir in oats, chocolate morsels, and pecans. Drop by tablespoonfuls onto greased (with shortening) baking sheets.

3. Bake at 350° for 12 minutes. Cool on baking sheets 3 minutes; remove to wire racks to cool completely.

BAKING SECRETS
from the Southern Living Test Kitchen

Lightly grease baking sheets only if the recipe specifies, and use only vegetable cooking spray or solid shortening. Butter or margarine encourages burning.

MARBLE SNICKERDOODLES

(pictured on page 251)

*Simple snickerdoodles get an upgrade with a swirl of chocolate cookie dough.
Cream of tartar may sound like a strange cookie ingredient, but don't
skip it—it gives snickerdoodles their unmistakable signature flavor.*

makes about 2½ dozen cookies   hands-on 45 min.   total 1 hour, 50 min.

3⅔ cups all-purpose flour
2½ tsp. cream of tartar
1½ tsp. baking soda
½ tsp. kosher salt
⅓ cup unsweetened cocoa
1¾ cups butter, softened

2½ tsp. vanilla extract
2⅓ cups sugar, divided
4 tsp. ground cinnamon, divided
3 large eggs
Parchment paper

1. Stir together 2 cups flour, 1¼ tsp. cream of tartar, ¾ tsp. baking soda, and ¼ tsp. salt in a medium bowl. Stir together cocoa and remaining 1⅔ cups flour, 1¼ tsp. cream of tartar, ¾ tsp. baking soda, and ¼ tsp. salt in another medium bowl.

2. Beat butter, vanilla, 2 cups sugar, and 1 tsp. cinnamon at medium speed with an electric mixer until creamy. Add eggs, 1 at a time, beating well after each addition. Spoon half of butter mixture into cocoa mixture; spoon remaining butter mixture into flour mixture.

3. Beat plain batter until just blended; beat chocolate batter until just blended. Chill both mixtures 30 minutes.

4. Preheat oven to 350°. Stir together remaining ⅓ cup sugar and 3 tsp. cinnamon in a small bowl. Drop plain dough by level tablespoonfuls onto aluminum foil. Top each with 1 Tbsp. chocolate dough; roll together into a ball. Roll in cinnamon-sugar; place 3 inches apart on parchment paper-lined baking sheets, and flatten.

5. Bake at 350° for 14 minutes or until edges are lightly browned, lightly tapping baking sheets halfway through to deflate cookies. Cool 5 minutes; transfer to wire racks, and cool.

×××××××××××××××××××××××××××××××××××

time-saving tip
Use the bottom of a ½-cup dry measuring cup
to flatten the cookies to the perfect size.

×××××××××××××××××××××××××××××××××××

GRANDMA'S TEA CAKES

Even though they're called cakes, tea cakes are simple Southern sugar cookies. The base ingredients generally include butter, sugar, eggs, flour, and vanilla, but many bakers have stirred in additional flavors to make their recipe their own, including spices such as allspice, cloves, and ground ginger.

makes about 6 dozen cookies   hands-on 30 min.   total 1 hour, 35 min.

1 cup butter, softened	1½ tsp. fresh lemon juice
1¼ cups sugar	3 large eggs
¾ cup cane syrup	4½ cups self-rising flour
1 Tbsp. vanilla extract	Parchment paper

1. Preheat oven to 350°. Beat butter and sugar at medium speed with an electric mixer until creamy. Add cane syrup and next 2 ingredients, beating just until blended. Add eggs, 1 at a time, beating just until blended after each addition. Gradually add flour, beating at low speed just until blended after each addition. Drop dough by rounded spoonfuls 2 inches apart onto parchment paper-lined baking sheets, using a small cookie scoop (about 1¼ inches).

2. Bake at 350° for 8 to 10 minutes or just until edges begin to turn golden brown. Cool on baking sheets on wire racks 1 minute; transfer to wire racks. Cool completely (about 15 minutes). Store in airtight containers 1 week.

Pecan Tea Cakes: Stir 1½ cups toasted chopped pecans into dough after adding flour in Step 1.

Snickerdoodle Tea Cakes: Stir 1½ tsp. ground cinnamon into flour before adding to butter mixture in Step 1. Stir together ⅔ cup sugar and 1 Tbsp. ground cinnamon in a shallow dish or pie plate; drop spoonfuls of dough into cinnamon-and-sugar mixture before placing on parchment paper-lined baking sheets. Bake as directed.

coconut

The large, husk-covered fruit of the palm tree, coconut has endless uses in both savory and sweet recipes. It's the extra touch that turns a bowl of fruit into ambrosia or takes cakes from weeknight to holiday. Fresh, canned, or frozen coconut is sold grated, shredded, and flaked in sweetened or unsweetened form. We're partial to toasting the large ribbon-like flakes to use as cake and cookie garnishes.

HUMMINGBIRD OATMEAL COOKIES

A new spin on the famed Hummingbird Cake that first appeared in the pages of Southern Living in 1978, there's no shortage of fruit in these cookies. They're filled with mashed bananas and pineapple, then topped with banana chips and coconut. No time for frosting? Bake anyway! We loved these plain too.

makes about 4 dozen cookies   hands-on 35 min.   total 1 hour, 37 min.

2 cups all-purpose flour	1½ cups uncooked regular oats
2 tsp. ground cinnamon	1 cup finely chopped pecans
1 tsp. baking soda	½ cup finely chopped dried pineapple
½ tsp. kosher salt	Parchment paper
1 cup butter, softened	Cream Cheese Frosting
1 cup firmly packed light brown sugar	½ cup chopped dried banana chips
1 tsp. vanilla extract	½ cup toasted sweetened flaked coconut
2 large eggs	½ cup toasted chopped pecans
½ medium-size ripe banana, mashed	

1. Preheat oven to 350°. Stir together first 4 ingredients in a medium bowl. Beat butter, brown sugar, and vanilla at medium speed with an electric mixer 3 to 5 minutes or until creamy. Add eggs, 1 at a time, beating well after each addition. Add flour mixture and banana; beat just until blended. Add oats and next 2 ingredients; stir until blended.

2. Drop dough by heaping tablespoonfuls 2 inches apart onto 2 parchment paper-lined baking sheets. Flatten each, using a lightly floured flat-bottomed glass.

3. Bake at 350° for 12 minutes or until golden. Cool on baking sheets 10 minutes; transfer to wire racks, and cool.

4. Spread Cream Cheese Frosting over each cookie; sprinkle with banana chips, coconut, and pecans, pressing to adhere.

CREAM CHEESE FROSTING

2 cups powdered sugar, sifted	½ tsp. kosher salt
4 oz. cream cheese, softened	¼ cup heavy cream
1 tsp. vanilla extract	

Beat powdered sugar, cream cheese, vanilla, and kosher salt at medium speed with an electric mixer 3 to 5 minutes or until smooth. Add cream, and beat until smooth.
Makes about 2 cups.

FRUITCAKE COOKIES

Chock-full of dried fruit and pecans, these chewy two-bite nibbles won't be relegated to the re-gift pile.

makes about 9 dozen cookies   hands-on 15 min.   total 53 min.

1½ cups sugar
1   cup butter, softened
3   large eggs
1   tsp. vanilla extract
3   cups all-purpose flour
1   tsp. baking soda

Pinch of table salt
1   lb. mixed candied fruit and peel
4   cups toasted chopped pecans
1   cup raisins
1   cup maraschino cherries, chopped

1. Preheat oven to 300°. Beat sugar and butter at medium speed with a heavy-duty electric stand mixer until creamy. Add eggs, 1 at a time, beating until blended after each addition. Stir in vanilla.

2. Sift together flour, baking soda, and salt; gradually add to sugar mixture, beating until blended. Stir in candied fruit and peel, pecans, raisins, and cherries. Drop dough by tablespoonfuls, 1 inch apart, onto lightly greased baking sheets.

3. Bake at 300° for 18 to 20 minutes or until lightly browned. Cool completely on wire racks (about 20 minutes).

xxxxxxxxxxxxxxxxxxxxxxxxxxxxxxxxxxxxxx

sweet idea

Turn these fruit-studded cookies into festive ice-cream
sandwiches by scooping ¼-cup scoops rum raisin
ice cream onto flat sides of half of cookies and topping with
remaining cookies. Freeze immediately for at least 2 hours,
then wrap in wax paper, and freeze until ready to serve.

xxxxxxxxxxxxxxxxxxxxxxxxxxxxxxxxxxxxxx

~ ginger ~

A tropical plant known for its gnarled, bumpy rhizome, gingerroot has a tan, thin skin and pale yellow flesh. Its flavor is peppery and slightly sweet, and it has a pungent, spicy aroma. While most familiar as the spice in gingerbread and the predominant flavor in gingerale, whether freshly grated or dried and ground, ginger can give life to many recipes, from cocktails and appetizers to stir-fries and baked goods.

HONEY~ORANGE~ GINGER COOKIES

By replacing some of the sugar with honey in this recipe, the spicy ginger flavor is mellowed and cookies take on a chewy texture.

makes about 4 dozen cookies   hands-on 25 min.   total 1 hour, 23 min.

⅔ cup sugar
½ cup butter, softened
½ cup honey
1 tsp. orange extract
1 large egg
2¼ cups all-purpose flour

1 Tbsp. loosely packed orange zest
1 tsp. ground ginger
½ tsp. baking soda
½ tsp. baking powder
Additional granulated sugar

1. Preheat oven to 350°. Beat sugar and butter at medium speed with a heavy-duty electric stand mixer until creamy. Add honey, orange extract, and egg, beating until blended.

2. Stir together flour, orange zest, ground ginger, baking soda, and baking powder; gradually add to sugar mixture, beating until blended. Cover and chill 30 minutes to 1 hour.

3. Shape dough into 1-inch balls; roll in sugar. Place 2 inches apart on ungreased baking sheets, and slightly flatten each with bottom of a glass.

4. Bake at 350° for 8 to 10 minutes or until lightly browned. Cool completely on wire racks (about 20 minutes).

BAKING SECRETS
from the Southern Living Test Kitchen

The flavor of dried and crystallized ginger is very different from fresh gingerroot, and they cannot be substituted for one another.

CANE SYRUP SLICE 'N' BAKES

Sweeter than molasses, cane syrup is a highly regarded Southern sweetener. This make-ahead cookie dough can be stored in the refrigerator up to one week or frozen up to one month.

makes about 5 dozen cookies   hands-on 35 min.   total 3 hours, 10 min.

2   cups butter, softened
¾   cup granulated sugar
¼   cup cane syrup*
1½ tsp. kosher salt
2   tsp. vanilla extract

4   cups all-purpose flour
1   large egg, lightly beaten
½   cup turbinado sugar
     (such as Sugar in the Raw)

Parchment paper

1. Beat first 5 ingredients at medium speed with an electric mixer 2 to 3 minutes or until creamy.

2. Add flour; beat until blended. Divide dough into 4 portions, and shape each portion into an 8- x 2-inch log. Wrap in plastic wrap, and chill 1 hour.

3. Whisk together egg and 1 Tbsp. water. Unwrap logs, and brush with beaten egg. Sprinkle turbinado sugar over logs, pressing to adhere, and rewrap. Chill 30 minutes.

4. Preheat oven to 350°. Cut logs into ¼-inch-thick slices; place 1 inch apart on 2 parchment paper-lined baking sheets. Bake at 350° for 10 to 14 minutes or until edges are lightly browned, switching pans halfway through. Cool on baking sheets 5 minutes. Transfer to wire racks, and cool.

* Sorghum syrup or honey may be substituted.

Black-Tie Benne Slice 'n' Bakes: Prepare recipe as directed, reducing butter to 1½ cups and adding ½ cup each tahini and white sesame seeds to first 5 ingredients in Step 1. Substitute ¾ cup black sesame seeds for turbinado sugar.

Gingersnap Slice 'n' Bakes: Prepare recipe as directed, reducing salt to 1¼ tsp. and adding 2 tsp. ground cinnamon, 1 tsp. ground cardamom, and ¼ tsp. each ground allspice, ground cloves, and ground nutmeg to first 5 ingredients. Stir in ½ cup chopped crystallized ginger after adding flour.

Fruitcake Slice 'n' Bakes: Soak 1 cup candied fruit, 1 tsp. firmly packed orange zest, and 1 tsp. loosely packed lemon zest in ¼ cup spiced or dark rum 30 minutes. Prepare recipe as directed, stirring fruit mixture into dough after adding flour. Substitute ¾ cup chopped walnuts for turbinado sugar.

Lemon-Rosemary Slice 'n' Bakes: Prepare recipe as directed, omitting egg and turbinado sugar and adding 1 Tbsp. loosely packed lemon zest and 2 tsp. minced fresh rosemary to first 5 ingredients. Reduce flour to 3½ cups, and add ½ cup cornmeal with flour. Gently toss together warm cookies and 2 cups powdered sugar to coat.

PARAGON
COMPOSITION
POKER CHIPS A.N.C.
TRADE MARK
No. S 508
Size 1⅝ in.
100

265

AMBROSIA MACAROONS

Classic Southern ambrosia has just four ingredients: oranges, coconut, sugar, and orange juice. But we have taken the "food of the Gods" from the fruit bowl to the cookie plate. Go for some glitz and glamour, and garnish these soft, chewy macaroons with candied fruit such as orange peel or red and green cherries.

makes about 6 dozen cookies   hands-on 20 min.   total 1 hour, 15 min.

1   large egg white
¼   cup sugar
¼   cup butter, melted and cooled
¼   cup fresh lime juice
1   tsp. loosely packed orange zest
½   tsp. vanilla extract
½   tsp. kosher salt

½   cup all-purpose flour
1   (14-oz.) package sweetened flaked coconut
½   cup finely diced dried pineapple
Parchment paper
36   red maraschino cherries, drained, halved, and patted dry

1. Preheat oven to 350°. Beat egg white at high speed with an electric stand mixer, using whisk attachment, until foamy; gradually add sugar, 1 Tbsp. at a time, beating until soft peaks form and sugar dissolves.

2. Gently stir in butter and next 4 ingredients. Stir in flour. Stir in coconut and pineapple until blended.

3. Drop batter by teaspoonfuls, 1 inch apart, onto 2 parchment paper-lined baking sheets. Place 1 cherry half in center of each cookie.

4. Bake at 350° for 12 to 15 minutes or until edges are golden brown, switching baking sheets halfway through. Cool on baking sheets 10 minutes; transfer cookies to wire racks, and cool.

BAKING SECRETS
from the Southern Living Test Kitchen
When baking more than one baking sheet of cookies at a time, be sure to rotate and turn baking sheets halfway through baking, so cookies brown evenly.

SUGAR COOKIE CUTOUTS

*Choose your favorite cookie cutters for these sugar cookies
to match any holiday or celebration.*

makes about 4 dozen cookies   hands-on 30 min.
total 2 hours, 30 min. (not including glaze)

4	cups all-purpose flour	2	tsp. vanilla extract
1	tsp. baking powder	2	large eggs
½	tsp. kosher salt		Parchment paper
2	cups granulated sugar		Chicory Coffee Glaze or Mulled Wine Glaze
1¼	cups butter, softened		

1. Stir together first 3 ingredients. Beat sugar and next 2 ingredients at medium speed with an electric mixer 2 to 3 minutes or until creamy. Add eggs, 1 at a time, beating after each addition. Gradually add flour mixture, beating just until blended.

2. Divide dough into 4 equal portions; flatten each into a ½-inch-thick disk. Wrap each in plastic wrap; chill 30 minutes. Working with 1 disk at a time, place on a lightly floured surface; roll to ¼-inch thickness. Cut with a 3-inch cutter. Place 1 inch apart on 2 parchment paper-lined baking sheets. Chill 30 minutes.

3. Preheat oven to 350°. Bake cookies at 350° for 10 minutes or until edges begin to brown, switching baking sheets halfway through. Cool on baking sheets 10 minutes; transfer to wire racks, and cool completely. Glaze as desired.

CHICORY COFFEE GLAZE

2	cups powdered sugar	2	Tbsp. whipping cream
2	Tbsp. strong brewed chicory coffee	¼	tsp. kosher salt

Stir together all ingredients until smooth. Stir in up to 2 tsp. water, 1 tsp. at a time, until desired consistency. **Makes about 1¼ cups.**

MULLED WINE GLAZE

1	cup red wine (such as Merlot)	⅛	tsp. ground nutmeg
1	Tbsp. light brown sugar	⅛	tsp. ground cinnamon
1	(4- x ½-inch) orange peel strip	¼	tsp. kosher salt
⅛	tsp. ground allspice	2	cups powdered sugar
⅛	tsp. ground cloves		

Bring wine, brown sugar, orange peel strip, ground allspice, ground cloves, ground nutmeg, and ground cinnamon to a boil in a saucepan over high heat; boil 7 to 10 minutes or until reduced to ¼ cup. Remove from heat, and stir in kosher salt until dissolved. Discard orange peel, and stir in powdered sugar until smooth. **Makes about 1¼ cups.**

PEPPERMINT CHOCOLATE LINZER COOKIES

Be sure to bake the cookies until they are crisp; the chocolate dough makes it harder to tell when they're fully cooked.

makes 2 dozen cookies   hands-on 45 min.   total 1 hour, 40 min.

3   cups all-purpose flour
1⅓ cups unsweetened cocoa
½   tsp. table salt
1   cup butter, softened
1   cup granulated sugar
½   cup firmly packed light brown sugar
1   Tbsp. instant coffee granules

2   tsp. vanilla extract
½   tsp. peppermint extract
2   large eggs
Parchment paper
1   cup crushed hard peppermint candies
Vanilla candy coating, melted

1. Stir together flour and next 2 ingredients. Beat butter and next 5 ingredients at medium speed with an electric mixer 3 to 4 minutes or until creamy. Add eggs, and beat until smooth. Add flour mixture, and beat just until blended.

2. Divide dough into 2 equal portions. Flatten into disks between parchment paper. Roll each to ¼-inch thickness; transfer to a baking sheet, and chill 30 minutes.

3. Preheat oven to 350°. Place 1 dough disk on work surface, and remove top sheet of parchment paper. Cut with a lightly floured 2½-inch round cutter, rerolling scraps once; place 1 inch apart on 2 parchment paper-lined baking sheets.

4. Cut centers out of half of cookies with a lightly floured 1½-inch round cutter. Sprinkle 1 tsp. crushed peppermint candies over each hollow cookie.

5. Bake at 350° for 12 minutes or until firm. Transfer cookies to a wire rack, and cool. Spread 1 tsp. melted candy coating onto solid cookies; top with hollow cookies.

XXXXXXXXXXXXXXXXXXXXXXXXXXXXXXXXXX

sweet idea

These festive sandwich cookies were made for sharing.
Once the candy coating has set, arrange cookies in
a decorative tin filled with holiday tissue paper.
In the covered tin, cookies should last up to a week.

XXXXXXXXXXXXXXXXXXXXXXXXXXXXXXXXXX

DOUBLE CHOCOLATE CHIP COOKIES WITH BOURBON GANACHE

*As if these cookies weren't decadent enough, we sandwiched
Bourbon Ganache between them for more wow!*

makes 2½ dozen cookies   hands-on 45 min.   total 5 hours, 48 min.

¾ cup butter, softened
¾ cup granulated sugar
¾ cup firmly packed dark brown sugar
2 large eggs
1½ tsp. vanilla extract
2½ cups all-purpose flour

1 tsp. baking soda
¾ tsp. table salt
1 (12-oz.) package semisweet
 chocolate morsels
Parchment paper
Bourbon Ganache

1. Preheat oven to 350°. Beat butter and sugars at medium speed with a heavy-duty electric stand mixer until creamy. Add eggs, 1 at a time, beating just until blended after each addition. Add vanilla, beating until blended.

2. Combine flour and next 2 ingredients in a small bowl; gradually add to butter mixture, beating at low speed just until blended. Stir in morsels just until combined. Drop dough by level spoonfuls onto parchment paper-lined baking sheets, using a small cookie scoop (about 1⅛ inches).

3. Bake at 350° for 12 minutes or until golden brown. Remove from baking sheets to wire racks, and cool completely (about 30 minutes).

4. Spread Bourbon Ganache on flat side of half of cookies (about 1 Tbsp. per cookie); top with remaining cookies. Cover and chill cookies 2 hours or until ganache is firm.

BOURBON GANACHE

1 (12-oz.) package semisweet chocolate
 morsels
½ cup whipping cream

3 Tbsp. bourbon
3 Tbsp. softened butter
½ tsp. vanilla extract

Microwave semisweet chocolate morsels and whipping cream in a 2-qt. microwave-safe bowl at HIGH 1½ to 2 minutes or until chocolate is melted and smooth, stirring at 30-second intervals. Whisk in bourbon, softened butter, and vanilla. Cover and chill, stirring occasionally, 1 hour and 30 minutes or until spreading consistency. **Makes 2½ cups.**

~ sweet potatoes ~

We Southerners love our sweet potatoes. We mash them into casseroles, and spoon them into pie shells. So it's no surprise we appreciate the moist sweetness they give to these Sweet Potato-Marshmallow Sandwich Cookies.

SWEET POTATO~ MARSHMALLOW SANDWICH COOKIES

What would the holidays be without sweet potatoes and marshmallows?
Now you can enjoy the tradition of that cherished duo
in creamy, buttery cookies filled with all the scents of the season.

makes 2½ dozen cookie sandwiches   hands-on 45 min.   total 2 hours

1	cup butter, softened	1	tsp. freshly grated nutmeg
¾	cup powdered sugar	¾	tsp. ground cardamom
¾	cup canned sweet potato puree	½	tsp. ground ginger
2	tsp. vanilla extract	½	tsp. ground cinnamon
2½	cups all-purpose flour		Wax and parchment paper
¼	tsp. baking powder	1	Tbsp. Demerara sugar
⅛	tsp. table salt		Marshmallow Filling

1. Beat butter at medium speed with an electric mixer until creamy. Gradually add ¾ cup powdered sugar, beating until smooth. Stir in sweet potato and 2 tsp. vanilla until blended.

2. Stir together flour and next 6 ingredients. Gradually add flour mixture to butter mixture, beating at low speed until blended.

3. Divide dough in half; flatten each into a disk. Roll each disk to ¼-inch thickness between 2 sheets of wax paper. Transfer dough, in wax paper, to a baking sheet; chill 1 hour.

4. Preheat oven to 350°. Working with 1 portion of dough at a time, remove top wax paper; cut with a 2-inch round cutter, rerolling dough scraps once. Place 1 inch apart on parchment paper-lined baking sheets; sprinkle with Demerara sugar.

5. Bake at 350° for 12 to 14 minutes or until edges are golden. Cool on baking sheets 1 minute; transfer to wire racks. Cool completely. Spread about 2 tsp. Marshmallow Filling between cooled shortbread rounds to form sandwiches. Store in airtight containers.

MARSHMALLOW FILLING

½	cup marshmallow crème	1¼	tsp. meringue powder
½	cup butter, softened	1	tsp. vanilla extract
2	cups powdered sugar		

Beat marshmallow crème and softened butter with a heavy-duty electric stand mixer at medium speed 2 minutes or until smooth; gradually add 2 cups powdered sugar. Add meringue powder, and beat at high speed 2 minutes or until fluffy. Stir in 1 tsp. vanilla. **Makes about 2 cups.**

Tex-Mex Brownies

Lemon-Almond Bars

Peppermint Divinity Bars

Blackberry-Limeade Bars

TEX-MEX BROWNIES

(pictured on page 276)

*These are not your mama's brownies. The subtle heat from ground
red pepper turns them into conversation starters.*

makes 2 dozen brownies   hands-on 25 min.   total 2 hours, 20 min.

1½ cups butter	½ tsp. kosher salt
1 (16-oz.) package bittersweet chocolate morsels	1 cup semisweet chocolate morsels
2 cups all-purpose flour	1 cup granulated sugar
2 tsp. baking powder	¾ cup firmly packed dark brown sugar
1 tsp. ground cinnamon	4 large eggs
½ to 1 tsp. ground red pepper	1½ Tbsp. vanilla extract
	Parchment paper

1. Preheat oven to 350°. Cook first 2 ingredients in a large heavy-duty saucepan over low heat, stirring occasionally, 8 to 10 minutes or until melted and smooth. Remove from heat; cool completely (about 20 minutes).

2. Meanwhile, whisk together flour and next 4 ingredients in a large bowl until blended; stir in semisweet chocolate morsels.

3. Whisk together granulated sugar and next 3 ingredients until smooth. Whisk in bittersweet chocolate mixture. Whisk chocolate mixture into flour mixture just until combined.

4. Line bottom and sides of a 13- x 9-inch pan with parchment paper, allowing 2 to 3 inches to extend over sides; lightly grease parchment paper. Pour batter into pan.

5. Bake at 350° for 35 to 40 minutes or until a wooden pick inserted in center comes out with a few moist crumbs. Cool in pan.

6. Lift mixture from pan, using parchment paper sides as handles; cut into squares.

×××××××××××××××××××××××××××××××××

sweet idea

Give these brownies the regal treatment they deserve
by turning them into frosting-filled brownie sandwiches.
Split each brownie horizontally, and sandwich 1 Tbsp.
store-bought chocolate frosting between top and bottom halves.

×××××××××××××××××××××××××××××××××

LEMON-ALMOND BARS

(pictured on page 276)

Traditional lemon bars get a crunchy twist with the addition of an almond crumble topping.

makes 32 bars   hands-on 30 min.   total 2 hours, 35 min.

2¾ cups granulated sugar, divided
¾ cup butter, softened
2 Tbsp. plus 1 tsp. loosely packed lemon zest, divided
3¼ cups all-purpose flour, divided
½ tsp. table salt, divided
Vegetable cooking spray

6 large eggs
¼ cup chopped crystallized ginger
1 tsp. baking powder
⅔ cup fresh lemon juice
¼ cup butter, melted
½ cup sliced almonds
Garnish: powdered sugar

1. Preheat oven to 350°. Beat ¼ cup granulated sugar, butter, and 1 tsp. zest at medium speed with a heavy-duty electric stand mixer 2 minutes or until creamy. Stir together 2 cups flour and ¼ tsp. salt. Gradually add to butter mixture, beating until just blended. Coat a 13- x 9-inch pan with cooking spray. Press dough into bottom of prepared pan. Chill 15 minutes.

2. Bake at 350° for 15 to 20 minutes or until lightly browned. Remove from oven; reduce oven temperature to 325°.

3. Whisk together eggs and 2 cups sugar. Process ginger and ½ cup flour in a food processor 1 minute or until ginger is finely chopped. Stir in baking powder. Whisk ginger mixture into egg mixture. Whisk in lemon juice and remaining 2 Tbsp. lemon zest; pour over crust.

4. Bake at 325° for 15 to 20 minutes or until filling is just set. Remove from oven.

5. Stir together remaining ¾ cup flour, ½ cup sugar, and ¼ tsp. salt in a small bowl. Stir in melted butter until well blended. Stir in almonds. Sprinkle over hot lemon mixture, and bake 20 to 25 more minutes or just until lightly golden. Cool completely in pan on a wire rack (about 1 hour). Cut into squares.

BAKING SECRETS
from the Southern Living Test Kitchen

For quick cleanup and easy serving, line the bottom and sides of the pan with foil before adding the dough.

BLACKBERRY~LIMEADE BARS

(pictured on page 277)

Use Key limes for the brightest flavor. These bars are best served chilled.

makes 16 (2-inch) bars   hands-on 15 min.   total 3 hours, 35 min.

Parchment paper
½   cup butter, softened
¼   cup sugar
1   cup all-purpose flour
¼   tsp. table salt
1½ cups sugar
½   cup all-purpose flour

1   Tbsp. loosely packed Key lime zest
¼   tsp. table salt
1   large egg
3   large egg whites
2   cups fresh blackberries
⅔   cup fresh Key lime juice

1. Preheat oven to 350°. Line bottom and sides of an 8-inch square pan with parchment paper, allowing 3 inches to extend over sides.

2. Beat softened butter and ¼ cup sugar at medium speed with an electric mixer until smooth. Stir together 1 cup flour and ¼ tsp. table salt; gradually add to butter mixture, beating at low speed just until blended after each addition. Press dough into bottom of prepared pan.

3. Bake at 350° for 20 to 25 minutes or until lightly browned.

4. Whisk together 1½ cups sugar, ½ cup flour, Key lime zest, and ¼ tsp. salt in a large bowl. Whisk in 1 egg and 3 egg whites just until blended.

5. Process blackberries in a blender until smooth. Pour pureed berries through a fine wire-mesh strainer into sugar mixture, discarding seeds; whisk in Key lime juice. Pour over warm crust; bake at 350° for 30 to 35 minutes or until center is set.

6. Cool on a wire rack 30 minutes. Cover with plastic wrap; chill 2 hours. Lift from pan, using parchment paper sides as handles. Cut into bars.

✕✕✕✕✕✕✕✕✕✕✕✕✕✕✕✕✕✕✕✕✕✕✕✕✕✕✕✕✕✕✕✕✕

time-saving tip
Rather than painstakingly juicing those tiny Key limes,
save time and energy by purchasing a bottle of Key lime
juice. While they are easy to zest, they are harder to juice,
and the bottled variety will work just fine in this recipe.

✕✕✕✕✕✕✕✕✕✕✕✕✕✕✕✕✕✕✕✕✕✕✕✕✕✕✕✕✕✕✕✕✕

PEPPERMINT DIVINITY BARS

(pictured on page 277)

Make this recipe all the way through without stopping, spreading the warm divinity onto a still-warm cookie base. If the divinity is too cool, it will tear the cookie base as you spread it.

makes 32 bars   hands-on 50 min.   total 2 hours, 10 min.

3   cups all-purpose flour
1   Tbsp. baking powder
1   tsp. kosher salt
1   vanilla bean
1¼ cups butter, softened
2   cups sugar, divided
Parchment paper

¼   cup light corn syrup
2   large egg whites
1   tsp. vanilla extract
¼   tsp. peppermint extract
¾   cup crushed hard peppermint candies, divided

1. Preheat oven to 375°. Stir together first 3 ingredients.

2. Split vanilla bean; scrape seeds into bowl of a heavy-duty electric stand mixer; discard bean. Add butter and 1 cup sugar; beat at medium speed 2 minutes or until creamy. Add flour mixture; beat until blended.

3. Line bottom and sides of a 13- x 9-inch pan with parchment paper, allowing 2 to 3 inches to extend over sides; lightly grease parchment paper. Press dough into bottom of prepared pan. Bake at 375° for 20 minutes or until edges are golden brown.

4. Meanwhile, stir together corn syrup, ¼ cup water, and remaining 1 cup sugar in a small saucepan over high heat, stirring just until sugar dissolves. Cook, without stirring, until a candy thermometer registers 250° (7 to 8 minutes).

5. While syrup cooks, beat egg whites at medium speed, using whisk attachment, until foamy.

6. When syrup reaches 250°, beat egg whites at medium-high speed until soft peaks form. While mixer is running, gradually add hot syrup to egg whites. Increase speed to high; beat until stiff peaks form. (Mixture should still be warm.) Add vanilla and peppermint extracts, and beat at medium speed just until combined. Fold in ½ cup peppermint candies.

7. Working quickly, spread mixture on warm cookie base, using a butter knife or offset spatula. Sprinkle with remaining ¼ cup crushed peppermints, and cool.

8. Lift mixture from pan, using parchment paper sides as handles; cut into bars.

CARAMEL~CHOCOLATE CHIP COOKIE BARS

Is it a cookie or a bar? Who cares?! It's filled with lots of chocolate morsels and finished with a caramel swirl that's baked right in. It's the ultimate crowd-pleaser.

makes 16 squares   hands-on 20 min.   total 1 hour, 55 min.

1½ cups all-purpose flour
½ tsp. baking powder
½ tsp. table salt
1½ cups firmly packed light brown sugar
¾ cup butter, softened

2 large eggs
1½ tsp. vanilla extract
½ cup milk chocolate morsels
½ cup caramel bits (or 12 caramels)
2 Tbsp. heavy cream

1. Preheat oven to 350°. Whisk together flour, baking powder, and salt.

2. Beat brown sugar and butter at medium speed with an electric mixer until fluffy. Add eggs, 1 at a time, beating until blended after each addition. Add vanilla, beating until blended.

3. Gradually add flour mixture, beating at low speed just until blended. Stir in milk chocolate morsels just until combined. Spread batter in a lightly greased 8-inch square pan.

4. Microwave caramel bits and cream in a microwave-safe bowl at HIGH 1 minute; stir. Continue to microwave at 30-second intervals, stirring until caramels melt and mixture is smooth. Pour caramel mixture over batter, and gently swirl with a knife.

5. Bake at 350° for 35 to 40 minutes or until a wooden pick inserted in center comes out clean. (Center will rise and fall while baking.) Cool completely in pan on a wire rack (about 1 hour) before cutting.

Note: We tested with Kraft Premium Caramel Bits.

BAKING SECRETS
from the Southern Living Test Kitchen

Whenever you're making brownies or a sticky bar dessert, follow this shortcut for removing and cutting up bars with ease. Before pouring in batter, line the pan with lightly greased aluminum foil and allow 3 inches extra to fall over the sides of the pan. When they're baked, you can just lift them out and slice them easily on a cutting board.

RASPBERRY CHOCOLATE MERINGUE BARS

What makes these bars truly special is the layer upon layer of contrasting flavors and textures. A cookie-like base topped with gooey jam and melty chocolate topped off with crispy, crunchy meringue. Grab a fork and dig into these divine treats.

makes 3 dozen bars   hands-on 25 min.   total 2 hours, 10 min.

1   cup butter, softened
1½ cups granulated sugar, divided
2   large egg yolks
2½ cups all-purpose flour
1   (10-oz.) jar seedless raspberry preserves

1   cup semisweet chocolate morsels
4   large egg whites, at room temperature
¼   tsp. table salt
2   cups finely chopped pecans, lightly toasted

1. Preheat oven to 350°. Line a 15- x 10-inch jelly-roll pan with aluminum foil, allowing 2 to 3 inches to extend over sides; lightly grease foil.

2. Beat butter and ½ cup sugar at medium speed with a heavy-duty electric stand mixer until well blended. Add egg yolks, and beat until combined. Gradually add flour, beating at low speed 1 to 2 minutes or just until combined. Press mixture onto bottom of prepared pan.

3. Bake at 350° for 15 to 20 minutes or until golden brown. Remove from oven, and spread preserves over crust. Sprinkle with chocolate morsels.

4. Beat egg whites and salt at high speed, using whisk attachment, until foamy. Gradually add remaining 1 cup sugar, 1 Tbsp. at a time, beating until stiff peaks form and sugar dissolves (about 2 to 4 minutes). Fold in pecans. Gently spread egg white mixture over chocolate mixture.

5. Bake at 350° for 30 to 35 minutes or until meringue is browned and crispy. Cool completely on a wire rack (1 hour). Cut into bars.

~ pimiento cheese ~

Affectionately called "the pâté of the South," pimiento cheese is the best thing to happen to the sandwich since, well, sliced bread. But you don't have to stop there. From appetizers all the way to baked goods, pimiento cheese will always be a crowd favorite. Spelled pimiento or pimento (both correct), this cheese concoction is as essential to our Southern identity as sweet tea. Dress it up or down, but be sure to use freshly shredded cheese. Trust us. That preshredded stuff just doesn't cut it.

PIMIENTO CHEESE GOUGÈRES

Stamp a Southern accent on this classic French hors d'oeuvre.

makes about 4½ dozen gougères   hands-on 30 min.   total 1 hour, 20 min.

½   cup butter, cut up
¾   tsp. kosher salt
1¼ cups all-purpose flour
1   (4-oz.) jar diced pimiento, drained
4   large eggs

1½ cups (6 oz.) finely shredded
     sharp Cheddar cheese
1½ tsp. Dijon mustard
¼   tsp. ground red pepper
Parchment paper

1. Preheat oven to 425°. Bring first 2 ingredients and 1 cup water to a rolling boil in a 3-qt. saucepan over medium heat; cook, stirring constantly, 1 minute. Add flour all at once, and beat vigorously with a wooden spoon 1 minute or until mixture is smooth and pulls away from sides of pan, forming a ball of dough. Reduce heat to low, and cook, stirring constantly, 2 minutes. (Dough will begin to dry out.) Remove from heat, and let stand 5 minutes.

2. Meanwhile, pat pimiento dry with paper towels, and finely chop.

3. Add eggs to dough, 1 at a time, stirring to blend after each addition. (If dough separates, don't worry. It will come back together.) Add pimiento, cheese, and next 2 ingredients; stir 2 minutes or until fully combined.

4. Drop half of dough by level tablespoonfuls, 1 inch apart, onto 2 parchment paper-lined baking sheets.

5. Bake at 425° for 10 minutes, placing 1 baking sheet on middle oven rack and other on lower oven rack. Reduce temperature to 325°, switch baking sheets, and bake 10 to 12 more minutes or until golden and crisp. Cool on baking sheets 5 minutes. Repeat procedure with remaining dough. Serve warm.

BAKING SECRETS
from the Southern Living Test Kitchen

You can use a piping bag with a ½-inch round tip or a zip-top plastic freezer bag with a corner snipped off to pipe the dough onto the baking sheets.

PEPPER JELLY PALMIERS

Party-staples pepper jelly and puff pastry just got more fun.
Try them in this flaky, sweet-and-savory pastry.

makes about 4 dozen palmiers   hands-on 20 min.   total 1 hour, 50 min.

1   (17.3-oz.) package frozen puff pastry
     sheets, thawed
Parchment paper
1   cup plus 2 Tbsp. finely shredded
     Parmesan cheese

6   Tbsp. chopped fresh chives
½   tsp. kosher salt
½   tsp. freshly ground black pepper
½   cup hot pepper jelly

1. Roll 1 pastry sheet into a 12- x 10-inch rectangle on lightly floured parchment paper. Sprinkle with half of cheese, 3 Tbsp. chives, and ¼ tsp. each salt and pepper. Roll up pastry, jelly-roll fashion, starting with each short side and ending at middle of pastry sheet. Wrap pastry tightly with parchment paper. Repeat procedure with remaining pastry sheet, cheese, chives, salt, and pepper. Freeze pastries 1 to 24 hours.

2. Preheat oven to 375°. Remove pastries from freezer, and let stand at room temperature 10 minutes. Cut each roll into ¼-inch-thick slices, and place on parchment paper-lined baking sheets.

3. Bake, in batches, at 375° for 20 minutes or until golden.

4. Microwave pepper jelly in a microwave-safe bowl at HIGH 1 minute. Spread ½ tsp. pepper jelly onto each palmier. Serve immediately.

XXXXXXXXXXXXXXXXXXXXXXXXXXXXXXXXXXX

time-saving tip

To make the recipe ahead, prepare through Step 1, and wrap
the dough in plastic wrap. Freeze up to 1 month. Proceed
with recipe in Step 2 about an hour before the party starts.

XXXXXXXXXXXXXXXXXXXXXXXXXXXXXXXXXXX

GIVEAWAY GUIDE

The best part of baking is sharing the fruits of your labor with loved ones. Whether the lucky recipient is a new neighbor, an old friend, or a family member, you'll want your baked goods to not only look their best, but also to stay fresh for a day or two. Follow our helpful tips and tricks for packaging up sweet treats and savory surprises.

sealed with love

Before packaging up any baked treats, be certain that they have cooled completely. If they are wrapped up while still warm, condensation will form on the inside of the packaging and cause treats to become soggy or even create mold. Once they are cool, wrap baked treats in wax paper, plastic wrap, or a plastic storage bag before decorating as desired so treats stay fresh for as long as possible.

small but mighty

Some baked goods are naturally individually sized, such as cookies and muffins. If you're making something larger, like a skillet of cornbread or quick bread, consider baking them in smaller vessels; just watch them in the oven because they may take less time to bake. Your recipe will create more than one gift, plus packaging is all the more adorable with tiny treats.

grand gestures

Sometimes a big cake or tart is exactly what the occasion calls for. When giving large desserts, be sure to place them in or on something sturdy like a platter, cake plate, or wooden box. With the additional weight, you wouldn't want to see your hard work fall to pieces.

a recipe for joy

Don't forget to attach a recipe card with your baked goods, affixed with a ribbon or some twine. For many people, the recipe can be even more precious than the treats themselves, so be sure to include it. Plus, a beautiful handwritten recipe card will dress up the look of your gift without much effort.

give a little more

Whenever giving baked goods, think about what accessories might be needed when enjoying the treat. With breads or muffins, some preserves and a small spreader would be a welcome surprise, or a metal server alongside a cake or pie. Of course, if you give the baked goods on a platter, a cake stand, or in a tin, know that the recipient will assume that it's part of the gift too.

INDEX

C

M

O

METRIC EQUIVALENTS

*The information in the following charts is provided
to help cooks outside the United States successfully use the
recipes in this book. All equivalents are approximate.*

EQUIVALENTS FOR DIFFERENT TYPES OF INGREDIENTS

Standard Cup	Fine Powder (ex. flour)	Grain (ex. rice)	Granular (ex. sugar)	Liquid Solids (ex. butter)	Liquid (ex. milk)
1	140 g	150 g	190 g	200 g	240 ml
¾	105 g	113 g	143 g	150 g	180 ml
⅔	93 g	100 g	125 g	133 g	160 ml
½	70 g	75 g	95 g	100 g	120 ml
⅓	47 g	50 g	63 g	67 g	80 ml
¼	35 g	38 g	48 g	50 g	60 ml
⅛	18 g	19 g	24 g	25 g	30 ml

LIQUID INGREDIENTS BY VOLUME

¼ tsp =				1 ml
½ tsp =				2 ml
1 tsp =				5 ml
3 tsp =	1 Tbsp =		½ fl oz =	15 ml
	2 Tbsp =	⅛ cup =	1 fl oz =	30 ml
	4 Tbsp =	¼ cup =	2 fl oz =	60 ml
	5⅓ Tbsp =	⅓ cup =	3 fl oz =	80 ml
	8 Tbsp =	½ cup =	4 fl oz =	120 ml
	10⅔ Tbsp =	⅔ cup =	5 fl oz =	160 ml
	12 Tbsp =	¾ cup =	6 fl oz =	180 ml
	16 Tbsp =	1 cup =	8 fl oz =	240 ml
	1 pt =	2 cups =	16 fl oz =	480 ml
	1 qt =	4 cups =	32 fl oz =	960 ml
			33 fl oz =	1000 ml = 1 l

DRY INGREDIENTS BY WEIGHT

(To convert ounces to grams, multiply the number of ounces by 30.)

1 oz	=	¹⁄₁₆ lb	=	30 g
4 oz	=	¼ lb	=	120 g
8 oz	=	½ lb	=	240 g
12 oz	=	¾ lb	=	360 g
16 oz	=	1 lb	=	480 g

LENGTH

(To convert inches to centimeters, multiply the number of inches by 2.5.)

1 in	= 2.5 cm					
6 in	= ½ ft	= 15 cm			
12 in	= 1 ft	= 30 cm			
36 in	= 3 ft	= 1 yd	= 90 cm	
40 in	= 100 cm	= 1 m			

COOKING/OVEN TEMPERATURES

	Fahrenheit	Celsius	Gas Mark
Freeze Water	32° F	0° C	
Room Temperature	68° F	20° C	
Boil Water	212° F	100° C	
Bake	325° F	160° C	3
	350° F	180° C	4
	375° F	190° C	5
	400° F	200° C	6
	425° F	220° C	7
	450° F	230° C	8
Broil			Grill

©2015 Time Inc. Books

Published by Oxmoor House, an imprint of Time Inc. Books
1271 Avenue of the Americas, New York, NY 10020

Senior Editor: Katherine Cobbs
Associate Editor: Allison Cox Vasquez
Assistant Project Editor: Lacie Pinyan
Editorial Assistant: April Smitherman
Senior Designer: Melissa Clark
Junior Designer: AnnaMaria Jacob
Executive Photography Director: Iain Bagwell
Photo Editor: Kellie Lindsey
Senior Photographer: Hélène Dujardin
Photographer: Greg DuPree
Senior Photo Stylists: Kay E. Clarke,
    Mindi Shapiro Levine
Photo Stylists: Ginny Branch, Mary Clayton Carl
Food Stylists: Victoria E. Cox, Margaret Monroe Dickey,
    Tami Hardeman, Stefanie Maloney,
    Catherine Crowell Steele
Test Kitchen Manager: Alyson Moreland Haynes
Senior Recipe Developer and Tester: Callie Nash
Assistant Production Director: Sue Chodakiewicz
Senior Production Manager: Greg A. Amason
Assistant Production Manager: Diane Rose Keener
Copy Editors: Donna Baldone, Rebecca Henderson
Proofreader: Rebecca Brennan
Indexer: Mary Ann Laurens
Fellows: Nicole Fisher, Amanda Widis

ISBN-13: 978-0-8487-4642-1
ISBN-10: 0-8487-4642-2
Library of Congress Control Number: 2015944367

Printed in the United States of America
10 9 8 7 6 5 4 3 2 1
First Printing 2015